BRAVE
LEADERSHIP
IS A
CHOICE

An Inclusive Guide to
Creating Belonging

CRYSTAL
WHITEAKER

Author: Crystal Whiteaker
Editor: Nailah Harvey
Cover design by: Mayanthi Jayawardena

Paperback ISBN: 979-8-9854578-1-0
E-Book ISBN: 979-8-9854578-2-7

For information on bulk purchases, licensing, workshops, and
guest speaking, visit BraveLeadershipChoice.com.

About Brave Leadership is a Choice: An Inclusive Guide to Creating Belonging

Brave Leadership is a Choice: An Inclusive Guide to Creating Belonging is for leaders who care deeply about cultivating inclusive, human-focused environments to support greater connection, creativity, and collaboration. Leaders will be guided through examining their roles in creating inclusive environments and learn how to:

- Get rooted in core values to make aligned decisions
- Identify and disrupt bias on personal, professional, and community levels
- Embody an inclusive leadership style that reflects their core values and how they want to support others
- Create a sense of belonging from within so more people feel brave enough to be who they are in the spaces they engage in
- Cultivate space for people to direct energy towards creativity, collaboration, and productivity, rather than worrying about whether or not they're welcome or belong in a space

*"**Brave Leadership is A Choice: An Inclusive Guide to Creating Belonging'** is extremely relevant and easily applicable in real-life work.* In my nearly 10 years working with the DEIB and HR departments of the corporate, private and nonprofit worlds, and having worked through many presentations and seminars on this subject, I have yet to see such an excellent distillation of this subject with focus on leadership."

–Laura Fennell, Director of Communications Strategy, Western Division; Anti-Defamation League

"Inclusion is a must for people to feel welcome and find a sense of belonging. It's not a fad! Our brains, bodies, and souls need to know that we are welcome and can be brave in order to put our best selves forward in any educational or business setting. The challenge? Learning what it means to be inclusive. **Crystal breaks down language, concepts and challenges in a way that allows anyone to learn what true inclusion is. Using the lens of identifying core values, it will challenge you to consider your biases and help you to attract the people you want in your community.** *The book allows you space to start exactly where you are without feeling judged. It's great for those who are just starting a journey to being aligned AND for those who have been doing the work for years."*

–Kirstie Wheeler, Educational Consultant and Associate Professor; Berklee College of Music

"Brave Leadership is A Choice is a wonderful book! It's beautiful. Fantastic. Informative. Insightful. Poignant. And important. It makes you want to go deeper into everything. I couldn't stop reading. Crystal shares specific stories and examples of personal experiences that connect you to the human experience and importance of safety and belonging. She provides real perspective on how to incorporate inclusive practices into our day-to-day lives to evolve as leaders. I loved it and wanted more!"

–Paige Ray, Founder, Commercial Photographer and Creative Director; Paige Ray Creative

DEDICATION

To my mom, Tamara. Thank you for seeing me, hearing me, and understanding me. I am so appreciative of our relationship and the time we have shared really getting to know one another. I am so proud of us for the healing work we have done and continue to do. I love you all the way to Saturn and back.

LAND ACKNOWLEDGMENT

I acknowledge the unceded land I occupy, where this book was written, belonged to Tongva, Kizh, and Chumash peoples.

If you aren't familiar, land or territory acknowledgements are a way of bringing awareness to the history of colonialism and honoring the Indigenous Peoples and native nations whom the stolen lands we occupy and gather on belonged to. You can visit native-land.ca to learn more about land acknowledgements. You can also enter your address to learn about the native tribes and Indigenous Peoples the land you occupy belonged to.

When we take time to acknowledge the harm of colonialism that Indigenous People have endured and continue to endure, we create space to recognize and honor the reality that even though we ourselves didn't create the disparities that exist, we are still a part of and operating within systems of oppression that continue to cause harm, with colonialism being one of the earliest, most harmful forms of trauma inflicted upon Indigenous Peoples.

TABLE OF CONTENTS

INTRODUCTION

"Change will not come if we wait for some other person or some other time. We are the ones we've been waiting for. We are the change that we seek."

–Barack Obama

I like to joke that I'm a corporate-trained creative hippie. If you scroll my Instagram feed, you'll notice saved live conversations and story highlights where I spent a lot of time in a hammock. Underneath my free-spirited persona is a wealth of knowledge and skills I picked up while working with directors of nonprofits and educational institutions, as well as the time I spent as an executive recruiter, vetting and recruiting director and C-level executives for placement in multi-million and billion dollar corporations across a range of industries. It was a lot like getting paid to get an MBA. The most common thing I recognized throughout my corporate career was minimal diversity at the leadership level. I often wondered why that was the case since there are so many smart, talented, capable individuals from a range of backgrounds and lived experiences that could contribute so much to workplace environments. When I think back on the behind-the-scenes access I had to participate in the hiring processes for leaders, hindsight leads me to ask 'what was the role of everyone involved–including myself–and how could we all have done better?'

In 2015, I finally acknowledged traditional corporate roles weren't for me. I felt drawn to explore my creative side and started freelancing as a photographer in Los Angeles. Then, in 2016 I left the corporate world to pursue contract work and give entrepreneurship a try. I built my photography portfolio by asking friends and friends of friends to model for me in exchange for photos. At the time, I didn't think about the fact that I had a rather diverse social circle. However, clients who hired me noticed and often commented that they appreciated the diversity represented. When I look back at my photography portfolio filled with people who trusted me enough to invite me in to photograph memorable, intimate parts of their lives, I see a range of human beings. I learned more about creating belonging through connecting with my clients than I ever could have imagined, had I stayed in corporate roles.

One of the most impactful, transformative experiences I can recall from a photo session was in 2018, during a trip to Havana, Cuba. The trip was a photo and art tour led by Amanda Bjorn, who introduced me to two of her friends, Felix and Ishak. They were celebrating their one-year anniversary and were excited about documenting the milestone. We met early on the morning of their photo session while the streets were clear and the city was quiet. They wore statement jackets and embodied stylish couple goals. The city streets of Havana provided a backdrop that was a colorful reminder of a place where art and creativity were abundant, but resources were not. This was one of several trips I had taken over the course of a year that reminded me of my own privileges, despite my marginalized identity. I was keenly aware of my surroundings as I captured the connection between Felix and Ishak. The energy flowed effortlessly as we worked together to create photographs that would end up being my first published photography session. Their images ended up in multiple LGBTQ+ inclusive publications, including my then favorite wedding industry publication, Catalyst Wedding Co. I remember the session clearly and while it was successful overall, there was one interaction that I won't ever forget. While Felix and Ishak were positioned in the street in a loving pose, someone walked by and heckled them in Spanish, prompting an angry reaction from Felix. I can still remember him saying people needed to mind their business and just let them be gay. Of course, I agreed. While I had already made it a point to make sure the people in front of my camera felt valued and supported for who they were, those moments reinforced how important it is to honor people's identity and their lived experience.

As I grew my photography business, I received more comments from clients and other photographers about how inclusive my portfolio was. I also received questions about how I was able to build such a diverse portfolio and attract more diverse clients, though commentary wasn't always positive. I remember the unnecessary comments from a woman at a bridal show in Orlando, Florida, who told me I shouldn't display photos of gay people at a bridal event. Nevermind that it was a 'bridal show' and not a 'wedding show.' Interactions like this made it clear to me that there was a need for education on building genuinely inclusive human-focused, core values-driven business practices. Especially in the wedding industry. In 2019, I began mentoring other photographers and creatives on how to incorporate inclusive practices into their businesses. By 2021, my mentoring services expanded to consulting with business owners across a range of specializations to help them dig into the core of who they are in each of the roles they occupy in their life. Now, I work with clients to get them rooted in their core values so they can create genuinely inclusive, welcoming environments and experiences through human-focused business practices. I've had clients who have been in business for a decade longer than I have who have shared that they've found more clarity, connectivity and authenticity through our work together than they ever had before. They've also shared that using my core values focused approach has helped them overcome their fears of saying or doing the wrong thing while incorporating inclusive practices; leading them to make more aligned decisions and book clients than they were before.

Diversity, equity, inclusion, and belonging (DEIB) work has come naturally to me, considering the most important piece of experience I can share that filters into my approach: my lived experience. I am a Black, bi-racial, queer woman who grew up in an all white family, in predominantly white, heteronormative communities and I didn't have any connection to the Black side of my heritage growing up. I always felt somewhat out of place and I didn't really have a true sense of belonging throughout most of my adolescence and early adulthood. Like many bi-racial people who are mixed with Black and white, growing up, I struggled with not feeling "white enough" or "Black enough." Being the only person of color in my family created a lot of confusion for me as a child. There is of course a lot of nuance in my lived experience and I want to be clear that I never felt unloved within my family, but I was keenly aware that I was different. I also didn't have the same privileges and access to resources that my white siblings did. I had to unlearn a lot of things that I internalized growing up because of the narratives and visuals I absorbed being the only Black girl, surrounded by white people, with no connection to the Black side of my heritage. I know what it feels like to wonder if I belong in a space and to feel uncomfortable talking about hard stuff with people I'm close to. I have a unique understanding of what is needed to create awareness and open up perspectives because I have learned how to navigate the world through multiple perspectives. This work is deeply personal to me. It is truly done out of love for myself and for the people and communities who deserve to have a sense of safety and belonging in the world. This is something I am very passionate about and I want us to do the work to normalize inclusion and value human-focused business so that it ripples through the environments we occupy.

I have worked 1-on-1 with dozens of leaders and entrepreneurs, and I have guided and trained hundreds of people through workshops and masterclasses using the key principles being covered in this book. I've been able to do this because of the experience I've gained throughout my unique personal and professional journey.

Why This Work Matters

"Inclusion is a hot topic right now."

I have lost count of the number of times a variation of this statement has been said in my presence. Statements like this occur so often that it's become challenging not to feel frustration. Incorporating behaviors, language, and practices intended to honor the humanity of marginalized people shouldn't be trendy.

In 2020, the world saw an awakening take place that led individuals and organizations to wake up the reality that it is long past time for people in positions of privilege to do better. Some have made a genuine effort, diving into the deep, uncomfortable end of the pool to do the necessary internal and external work. Others have hung out in the shallows seeking simple solutions they can use to show that they support diversity. And therein lies the problem. Supporting diversity is not the same as practicing inclusion. As organizations have moved to incorporate diversity through messaging and visuals, what they have failed to realize is that they often cause more harm than good through the exploitation of people from marginalized communities. Most of the time, those people are Black women.

Scholar-Activist, Public Speaker and Cultural Consultant, Dr. Yaba Blay (she/her) shared her experience on social media of being approached by a large TV network seeking to share stories in celebration of Juneteenth 2021. Dr. Blay was asked to write an essay about what Juneteenth meant to her. What she shared was a reflection of her experience around Juneteenth 2020, when she was inundated with requests to host workshops and conduct trainings about anti-racism. She was even approached many times by Corporate America to write statements condemning racism and standing in solidarity with the Black community. (Statements she refused to write.) Dr. Blay further shared that her essay had been edited to exclude the truth about being approached by Corporate America, seemingly because it didn't fit the narrative the TV network wanted to portray. The point Dr. Blay shared is that corporations, networks, and any organization with predominantly white populations and leadership that uphold capitalism only want to celebrate Black and marginalized communities when it benefits them; and they will exploit people (often Black women) for recognition and revenue-generating labor.

The experience shared by Dr. Blay is only one of many. And for anyone doing anti-racism and inclusion work, it is a very familiar scenario. It is not enough to simply support diversity and invite people from marginalized communities to do work for or within an organization. Practicing genuine inclusion isn't something that you buy in a package with a checklist, employ with a gallery of stock photos showing people from diverse backgrounds, or achieve by hiring people of color to write statements for you. Real change isn't made through external performative actions. Real change starts within. Genuine inclusion takes work—deep, uncomfortable, disruptive, work—and here is the truth: a lot of people in positions of privilege aren't yet ready to let go of their comfort to do the real work that's required of them in order to examine their participation in the oppressive, capitalist, patriarchal, white supremacist system that rules so much of our lives— yes, even our businesses and educational institutions. This is a system that people from marginalized communities have learned how to operate in just to *survive*.

Human beings and their lived experiences aren't a trend. People from marginalized communities deserve to thrive. When we create genuinely inclusive environments where people can feel a sense of belonging without spending mental and emotional energy wondering if they're actually welcome, that energy can be redirected to connection, creativity, and collaboration, which ultimately benefits all of us.

How This Book Came to Be

Brave Leadership is a Choice: An Inclusive Guide to Creating Belonging has, in many ways, been three decades in the making. The content was seeded through The Aligned Values Framework™ I developed that has been used with 1-on-1 clients, in masterclasses, and workshops from 2019 to 2021. I began the formal writing process in May 2021 and by July 2021, I realized I had more of my own internal work to do before I could continue. I took several months away from writing this book to focus on furthering my own healing while simultaneously supporting clients and growing my business. Writing this book has been an absolute labor of love as I've worked to heal my own wounds from heteronormative, patriarchal, white supremacist culture while creating resources and holding space to support people during their own journeys. Clients continuously share their appreciation for my approach to this work and how beneficial it is for anyone who engages with it. My approach is informed by my own intersectional identity and lived experience with a deep focus on core values, examining bias on multiple levels, and creating belonging from within. The Aligned Values Framework™ is designed to help you:

- *Clarify* your understanding of inclusion
- *Connect* to create belonging from within

- *Root* in your role, core values, and commitments
- *Disrupt* and identify bias on personal, professional, and community levels
- *Embody* a leadership style that reflects your core values
- *Create* genuinely inclusive environments and aligned relationships

I cannot work directly with everyone who would like to utilize my framework, so this book is an accessible resource for people who make the brave choice to take on any leadership role where they want to incorporate genuinely inclusive practices to create belonging for the people they engage with.

Who This Book is Written *To* and Who This Book is Intended to *Support*

This book is written to the brave leader who:

- Believes in leading with a human-focused approach
- Chooses to advocate for people from marginalized communities with less social privilege than themselves
- Wants to connect with themselves to create belonging from within
- Is committed to co-creating genuinely inclusive environments where all people can find a sense of belonging without having to change or segment parts of themselves to fit in

Ultimately, this book is intended to support people who are a part of marginalized groups through the advocacy of the brave leaders who commit themselves to doing the work to disrupt the status quo.

Brave Leadership is A Choice: An Inclusive Guide to Creating Belonging is for You if...

- You are committed to learning about ways to integrate practices to support diversity, equity, inclusion, and belonging
- You are aware of the general social disparities that exist between white and non-white people, heterosexual and LGBTQ+ people, able-bodied and disabled people
- You are aware that systemic oppression exists and the ideologies of white supremacy uphold systemic oppression
- You're seeking sustainable solutions that will help you integrate more inclusive practices, rather than a quick fix
- You believe you can make a difference

How to Engage with This Book

You are invited to do this work with a judgment-free perspective as you navigate the process of incorporating the tools you need to be a truly empowered, inclusive, welcoming leader to all. You are invited to take care of yourself as you work through any discomfort while incorporating the knowledge and tools you need to build an inclusive, human-focused leadership approach to your personal and professional life. This book was written to help you strengthen your leadership approach, not bring shame to previous decisions you've made in your role(s) personally or professionally.

You will be guided through the obvious and not-so-obvious elements of what it means to be an aligned, brave, inclusive leader. Some of the questions and exercises may feel uncomfortable, but that feeling is completely normal. It's important to work through the discomfort in order to understand why you feel the way you do so you can move toward inclusive, mindful awareness. By the end, you will have the tools to create a clearly defined personal philosophy that not only feels aligned to you, but also inspires others because you're going to work through your role and core values as a leader with mindful intention.

This is your opportunity to make a commitment to yourself and the people in your personal and professional social environments that make up your community. Are you ready to commit to showing up wholeheartedly to do the work every day to ensure you lead with curiosity to grow and co-create with people around you? Are you ready to ensure that the social environments you're a part of are truly inclusive and welcoming to all people? Some things may come more easily than others throughout this book and that's okay. The effort you put in will be worth it.

Setting Brave Intentions

It's important to make sure that you take time to create space for yourself that feels safe and comfortable to you as you engage with this material. I want to invite you to be brave enough to honor your humanity and your lived experience without guilt, shame, or judgment.

I want to invite you to make sure you have what you need to:

- Be present and engaged each time you pick up *Brave Leadership is A Choice*
- Make sure you're in a place where you can ground yourself so you're calm and regulated
- Give yourself permission to be honest, feel your feelings, and process anything that comes up
- Move through this work in a way that honors your energy

Honoring your needs while engaging in this work will help you remain committed since caring for yourself is a compassionate practice. Practicing self-compassion reminds us to also have compassion for others.

You're also invited to share a similar reminder for anyone you work with, if you hold space for people in any way. It's easy for us to get caught up in moving through things quickly without taking time to check in with ourselves. Sharing reminders with people to honor their energy is a human-focused practice that helps support your connections because you're taking the time to let people know that you care about their wellbeing.

If you're ready to commit, *Brave Leadership is A Choice: An Inclusive Guide to Belonging* is for you!

I (name) _____ am committed to showing up wholeheartedly for myself and the people who are a part of the social environments I participate in, personally and professionally, to ensure that my community is a true representation of my core values, starting today, (date) _____.

CHAPTER 1

Clarify Inclusion

"Inclusion is not bringing people into what already exists; it is making a new space, a better space for everyone."

—George Dei

Welcome to the work. I hope you're ready. Perhaps you're already on the journey to incorporating inclusive practices, or maybe you're just getting started. Either way, you understand that inclusion is important and all human beings deserve to be valued and feel a sense of belonging. Through the experiences I've shared engaging in this work with clients, I have been told repeatedly that having an initial understanding of words and phrases used to describe the experiences of marginalized people is the most helpful to start with when engaging in this work. This is why I've provided a glossary of key terms and definitions for you to reference in the back of this book. If you haven't already done so, I recommend pausing to read through the glossary first. Personally, this makes sense to me because I'm the type of person who likes to be able to name and define a thing or a feeling. Naming things offers a better understanding of what is taking place so we can find ways to move forward.

Understanding is ultimately what helps us make decisions for ourselves and the more clearly we understand things, the more confident we become. This is important to note because when we consider people who dismiss, disregard, invalidate, and harm other human beings because of who they are or what they believe, we learn that those people are often operating from a place of fear—not confidence—because they don't understand the lived experience of the human they're harming. People who inflict harm are often more afraid that the human with an experience they cannot relate to or understand is going to cause some sort of harm to *them*, so in turn, these people act in ways that are harmful towards human beings from marginalized communities because they believe they're protecting themselves and their loved ones. An example of harmful behavior from a place of fear, rather than understanding, plays out in scenarios where people who aren't supportive of the LGBTQ+ community engage in sharing hateful rhetoric or stating that they don't believe storylines involving LGBTQ+ people should be shown in media because they fear it could influence children and 'make them gay.' If this logic were factual and relationships portrayed in media dictated people's feelings of attraction, then people who identify as LGBTQ+ and were raised in heteronormative environments, with little to no access to LGBTQ+ media, would identify as heterosexual.

When you operate from a place of understanding, you're able to bring more compassion to a situation to help build confidence within yourself and the people around you. When you're able to engage with another human being from a place of understanding and compassion, you're creating a space of support for the other person, which allows them to access their own internal sense of safety and feel confident in who they are. As a result, you're able to hold that space and connect on a human level because neither of you feels the need to defend your perspective or experience. You're both allowing yourselves to be who you are. Inclusion is present when you and the people around you are free to be who you truly are. For clarity, let's make sure we're on the same page regarding the definition of inclusion, since that is the focus of this book. I like to use the definition from Oxford Languages which states that "inclusion is the practice or policy of providing equal access to opportunities and resources for people who might otherwise be excluded or marginalized."

When you read the definitions for *diversity, representation,* and *inclusion,* these words all seem to have a similar meaning; however, when applied to organizational structures and social environments, diversity and representation can quickly become meaningless if the organization isn't truly welcoming towards the groups they're outwardly trying to show representation for. This is also where tokenizing people and cultural appropriation can show up. How might this take shape?

Here are three fictional examples featuring diversity without representation or inclusion, tokenism, and cultural appropriation.

Example One – Diversity without representation or inclusion: If an organization with an all-white, male leadership team hires an LGBTQ+ person and two Black team members, they have diversified their team. If the same organization plans a company retreat on a plantation run by openly anti-LGBTQ+ business owners, the organization isn't considering the employees hired to diversify the team. By choosing a plantation as the location for the company retreat, the organization is sending a message to the Black employees that they did not consider how the dark history of a plantation could negatively impact them. In addition, the comfort and safety of the LGBTQ+ team member is compromised. Finally, the lack of diversity within the leadership team is a lack of representation for the employees of the organization.

Example Two – Representative tokenism without inclusion: An organization wants to show support for the LGBTQ+ community during Pride Month. They create a visual campaign showing people who appear to be part of the community, complete with rainbow flags and props. The organization uses the images created across their website, blog, and social media channels during Pride Month and then returns to business as usual the following months, where support for the community isn't continuous. The organization failed to practice genuine inclusion in this scenario by tokenizing people to represent the LGBTQ+ community in a marketing campaign without doing anything to actually support the community throughout the rest of the calendar year.

Example Three – Cultural appropriation: An event planning company is hired to put together a "Chinese New Year" themed party. The client who is hosting the party is not Chinese and has no ties to Chinese culture. The event planning staff has no ties to Chinese culture either, but they move forward with planning the event. No research or understanding of Chinese culture is considered and the client and the event planning team incorporate a mixture of decorations, costumes for guests, props, and catering staff dressed in Chinese garments to bring the event to life. However, much of what they do is rooted in stereotypes. The event planning company later shares photos of the event to further promote their services on social media, only to receive backlash for cultural appropriation. This happened because neither the client, nor any of their guests, had ties to Chinese culture. This also happened because the chosen theme was based on actual traditions from another culture without any understanding of its true meaning and rituals; it was deemed offensive.

From the three examples provided, consider this perspective: Diversity brings people in, representation gives them a voice, and inclusion makes them feel welcome, heard, and understood. When you bring people in and call it diversity, you're essentially giving people a seat at the table. It's only a start to the work. When you pay attention to the voices of people with different lived experiences, you're creating space for diverse solutions. It's a step forward. Making people feel welcome, heard, and understood lets them know that you're not just advocating for them. You're also connecting with them from a place of compassion.

Welcoming, listening, and learning to understand people is where change begins to take hold. Understanding leads to belonging and that's ultimately what people desire–to belong. Not fit in, but belong. There is a difference. Fitting in requires people to assimilate. Belonging allows space for people to be their whole, entire human selves. I share a visualization exercise at BraveLeadershipChoice.com that invites you to think about your experience with belonging and not belonging. When spaces are genuinely inclusive, people won't have to spend as much energy wondering if they're actually welcome and that energy can be redirected to creativity and collaboration, which is great for team leaders and businesses. Society is evolving and so are people's expectations of how they deserve to be treated, particularly people who are a part of marginalized communities.

Your understanding of inclusion and the role it plays in your behaviors and beliefs has the power to impact people regardless of whether or not you ever personally connect with them. Therefore, it's important to consider what someone's perception might be when they interact with you. Read that again. Notice how I stated 'whether or not you ever *personally connect* with them' and to 'consider what someone's perception might be when they *interact* with you?' This is important to recognize because you may interact with people whom you never personally connect with, but you could have a lasting impact on them. If you want to make a positive impact, you need to do the work to understand the realities of people's lived experiences. This starts with getting familiar with the language and phrases used to define those experiences. Now, I want to be clear, when I say inclusion, I'm not just talking about race. I'm considering people from all marginalized groups. While this book is primarily geared towards white, heterosexual people, it is still for all people because we *all* have work to do...straight, white people often have more to unpack and unlearn.

In case you're a heterosexual, white person reading this, wondering why people who share your demographics have the most to unpack and unlearn, simply put, it's because straight white people hold the most social power and privilege within the structure of white supremacy. We will cover this more in <u>Chapter 3: Root, Role, and Identity.</u>

Inclusion requires being open and mindful through learning and unlearning what is truly welcoming to all people. It requires you to form awareness from within yourself and the role you play in your life, whether you're a leader, educator, employee, parent, friend, etc. Inclusion carries through the connections that make up your community.

Tanisha Rodriguez (she/her), MSM Head of People and Culture Entropico—and President and Founder of Sister Circle Media—shared her perspective in relation to being mindful of others and determining whether people are being genuine:

> "I'm always about meeting people where they are so you can have a common language. When I first come to a project that wants my input, I like to know who the players are. How do they understand what I do? And what personal or professional work have they done? [I need to understand this] before we even get to the work. We won't be able to understand each other if we aren't speaking the same language. So, meet people where they are so you can have a common language.
>
> We can't control how others will receive the work because of [their unique] lived experiences and where they are in their lives now. All we can do is come to it as humble learners and collaborators. No one knows everything about DEIB. Hell, we can't even agree on an acronym! That's because we all need different things. This is why sometimes when white people do

something that they thought was great for Black people or a marginalized group and the [receiving] group is like *why did you do that?*, more issues arise because everyone is different and experiences things differently. This is why we need to be curious about learning and collaborating. I think you'll have a better chance of the experience being seen and felt as genuine."

If you want people to trust that you, as an individual, are truly inclusive, you have to be able to naturally communicate that you welcome all people on a regular basis through your words, actions, and behaviors. As you do this work, you'll need to prepare to do things that will require you to reconsider the way you operate and show up in the world. You will likely feel uncomfortable, personally attacked, guilty, angry, sad, ashamed, disconnected, and worried about whether or not you will be able to do anything "right." I don't tell you this to discourage you, but to prepare you so that you can begin implementing any strategies or practices that will help you manage your energy and engage in the work at a sustainable pace. Don't quit when it feels hard. Simply take a break, get a snack, and pick up where you left off.

Consider these three essential elements required for practicing inclusion: trust, compassion, and community.

Trust is the first element because people need to feel that they can trust what you say and do and that you are in integrity with what you share. If trust isn't established, or if trust is broken, a lack of safety is born. People need to feel safe in order to exist wholly and comfortably. It's also important to note that trust cannot be assumed. It has to be built. As Katie Kurtz, trauma informed social worker and author of the Trauma Competencies™ Framework and Trauma Informed Space Holding (TISH) Blueprint™ states: *"Trust is not assumed, it's cultivated. What may feel safe for me, may not feel safe for you."* This is also why it's necessary to shift language from *safe space* to *brave space*, which I cover in Chapter 2: Creating Mindful Connections.

Think about the last time you intuitively felt that someone was untrustworthy. Sit with that feeling. Recognize what the memory of it feels like. Next, think about someone you trust deeply and how that feels. Ideally, you experience an ease and comfort when you think about the person you trust deeply. Notice the opposing feelings that occur in your body when you think about these two people. Lastly, think about the last time you experienced having your trust broken, unexpectedly. What did that feel like? How did it affect the way you viewed that person? You're probably experiencing a mixture of feelings as you think about these memories. Pay attention to the differences because this will help you remain mindful of the importance of remaining in integrity with what you share and commit to so that people feel safe putting their trust in you. When people and communities recognize you to be trustworthy, you're going to receive invitations to spaces where your compassion is required.

Compassion is necessary because we have to acknowledge the fact that everyone has a different lived experience, particularly people who are a part of marginalized communities. There is also nuance when you consider the majority of marginalized people also hold multiple intersections in their lived experience. I share examples of this in Chapter 3: Root, Role, Identity, and Privilege. Understanding this and coming from a place of compassion when you're among people who have a different experience than you is required if you're going to make genuine connections and show up in a way that is truly supportive of the people and communities who need you. Yes, you read that right. Marginalized people need you, particularly if you have more social power, privilege, and influence. You can use your social privilege to influence other people with social privilege to practice more compassion and understanding. Holding people in compassion is a gift every human must learn to share if we're going to build a more equitable world. This is where community comes in since this work is most effective when there is a collective effort.

Community matters. The community we surround ourselves with and invest our time and energy in is a reflection of who we are and what we believe. When you think about the people who surround you, what types of people are included in that community? What do they care about? Are they working to practice inclusion themselves? Do you like what you see or are there red flags?

When it comes to inclusion work, having a strong, supportive, aligned community is necessary to raise collective awareness. When a community operates in unison towards the same goal, the outcome benefits everyone.

When you create genuinely inclusive environments, you're creating brave spaces that communicate to people you've taken the time to consider that the world—and the places you work in—are made up of many different people. You demonstrate that you care about truly connecting with people for who they are and the value they have as a human being. When people can imagine themselves in an environment where they feel welcome and connected, it helps build trust. When there is trust and confidence within your environment, people are more likely to want to work with you as opposed to another individual or organization who hasn't taken the time to ensure their environment is actually welcoming to all people.

Attracting dream connections and relationships—whether it's clients, network partners, or talent for your team—is the ultimate goal. The language and narrative you put out is what draws people in or turns them away. Genuine inclusion helps create an environment that allows room for more creative thinking and collaboration because people are less worried about whether or not they're welcome, and they are more focused on sharing their talents. When you work to ensure your environments are inclusive, it adds another layer of trust within your community.

Actionable Reflections:

The three essential elements for practicing inclusion are:
1. Trust
2. Compassion
3. Community

How can you honor these traits as a leader?

_____

_____

_____

_____

_____

_____

_____

_____

_____

_____

_____

_____

CHAPTER 2

Creating Mindful Connections

"I've learned that people will forget what you said, people will forget what you did, but people will never forget how you made them feel."

—Maya Angelou

You have the power to impact people regardless of whether or not you ever personally connect with them, so it's important to consider how you want people to experience you. I want to reframe something for you in terms of the way you view your business and professional environments: Businesses and professional environments are social, relational environments. Typically, businesses are viewed as professional environments and social environments have been considered separate spaces from work environments. But the reality is, our professional environments are social environments. Why? Because we interact with other human beings. Whether you work with people in person or online, those are human interactions. This includes the comments on social media. This is why, even within a professional environment, you're still creating a social, relational environment.

Social environment refers to the physical and social settings where people live, work, learn, and interact with individuals or groups of people. Healthy social environments are brave spaces that allow room for curiosity, open communication, learning, growth, creativity, collaboration, feedback, and belonging.

Inclusion in social environments goes beyond diversity and representation. It requires being open and mindful through learning and unlearning what is truly welcoming to all people. Awareness from within yourself in your role(s) and way of being, awareness for the people you collaborate with, and awareness of the connections that make up your community are vital in creating environments that offer a sense of safety and belonging for people. So think about the type of social environment you want to create within and around the role you're in. Think about how you want people to feel when they interact with you or see the way your existing community communicates in your comment threads online. You might be awesome, but if there are people in your comments being harmful towards others without being called in to examine their behavior, that's not going to show a very safe, supportive community space. And all of this trickles over into our personal environments, too. I don't subscribe to the school of thought that we leave everything at their respective doors, such as leaving personal stuff at the door when we get to work or leaving work stuff at the door when we get home. We're humans not robots. No matter how much we try to create separation, all of the environments we engage in will have an impact on us and influence how we show up wherever we go. I'm not saying you need to share all of your personal experiences with your team at work. Generally speaking, if you have a lot going on at home and it's impacting how you function at work, simply making your team aware of the reality that you're dealing with a lot will remind them you're human, create opportunities for connection, and give you the chance to ask for support. This can also help cultivate a more brave space.

In order to connect with people in a genuinely welcoming way, you'll need to clarify your personal mission, vision, and philosophy. Your personal mission is what drives you forward and keeps you going. It's how you describe what you value and who you're willing to show up for. Your vision is who you want to become. To formulate this, you'll need to revisit your core values, role, and your purpose within the social environments you participate in. Before you can develop (or revisit) your personal philosophy, it's important to understand the role(s) you occupy in social environments and the place inclusion has in your personal narrative. Impactful connections are made when you're clear on who you are, the mission that drives you, the vision you hold, and the philosophies you believe in. You can download a free guide on How to Create An Inclusive Personal Philosophy Statement at BraveLeadershipChoice.com to get started.

Brave Space vs. Safe Space:

As I shared what I learned from Katie Kurtz in Chapter 1: Clarify Inclusion, we cannot assume what feels safe for another person. The goal is for people to feel safe, however, the feeling of safety cannot exist in spaces where people don't have the ability to bravely show up wholly in their humanity or speak up and advocate for themselves or others. For this reason, you may notice the words 'brave' and 'safe' used interchangeably throughout this book. To avoid confusion, I want to clarify that helping people feel safe is the goal, however, all you or I can do at any time is create a brave space. Ideally, when you engage in this work, you will use the tools you gain to create brave spaces where people can feel safe enough to exist wholly in their humanity. When people are included and they feel a genuine sense of connection and belonging within the social environments they participate in, they are more willing to engage and feel empowered to show up as their whole, true selves. Having the ability to be whole in their humanity helps create a braver, safer social environment where there is less worry about being accepted and more space for connection, creativity, and collaboration.

Making genuine commitments to inclusion and continuously practicing them in the social environments you participate in is vital. Showing support for the Black community, the LGBTQ+ community, or the Indigenous People and People of Color, as well as people with disabilities, must extend beyond the days and months they're recognized and celebrated on the calendar each year. If you haven't previously felt comfortable talking about or examining your position on social issues, human rights, and equality, ask yourself why. Get into the discomfort and be honest with yourself about your thoughts and feelings when it comes to diversity, representation, and inclusion. One of the most common things people share when we work together is their surprise in response to the many words and phrases there are to describe behaviors and experiences that negatively impact marginalized people. Being surprised is often accompanied by feelings of internalized guilt, shame, or judgment, because they think *"How could I not know this?"* or *"Oh my goodness, I've done this!"* And I have to remind them it's not their fault that we all live and operate in a culture run by oppressive beliefs and systems. Even I have been surprised as a Black, bi-racial, queer woman when things I've done or experienced personally are named. I'm also aware this is a side effect of growing up in predominantly white, heteronormative communities where there were fewer conversations about marginalized experiences. Because how do you talk about things you don't understand? Oppressive systems don't want people to have knowledge and understanding because when we're able to name things, we can address it and do the necessary work to change it. This is one of the reasons why certain books are being banned in schools. Educating young people about the truth of oppression and the varied lived experiences of BIPOC, LGBTQ+ people and brave disruptors challenges the status quo. When you're engaging in this work, ask yourself if it's a singular thing you're not comfortable with or if it's many things. For example, if you're comfortable speaking on women's rights or LGBTQ+ rights, but you're not comfortable speaking about race, ask yourself why.

Below is a list of commitments and practices to incorporate to help make the social environments you participate in truly inclusive. It's important to remember that *you* have to practice inclusion as an individual and lead by example in your role(s). When you incorporate inclusive practices, you naturally communicate that all people are welcome to show up bravely in your presence on a regular basis through your words, actions, and behaviors. This includes:

- Sharing your commitment to inclusion with your team and your community
- Being mindful of the words you use
- Not placing expectations on people from marginalized groups to provide education if it's not their role
- Avoiding cultural appropriation and tokenizing people from marginalized groups.
- Advocating for accessibility for people with disabilities
- Seeking to understand people who are actually a part of the communities you strive to connect with
- Getting involved by supporting causes, participating in communities, and using your role and influence to elevate the people and causes you support
- Taking care of yourself and your energy when engaging in this work. If it feels necessary, consider taking space from people in your current community if they continue to cause harm and aren't open to listening. If you are operating from a truly inclusive perspective, taking

space from people who don't share those values will make room for more open-minded people

I realize the last suggestion in that list may be met with resistance. That's understandable. It's natural to feel resistance when you find that you're no longer aligned with people who have been part of your life after you evaluate your core values and beliefs. This part of committing to inclusion is always challenging. I've mourned multiple relationships over the years as I've come to terms with the reality that not everyone is ready to take the same journey, but I'm also learning to remain open to these same relationships should they ever decide to understand more about the lived experiences of marginalized people.

Actionable Reflections:

- You have the power to impact people regardless of whether or not you ever personally connect with them, so it's important to consider how you want people to experience you.
- Businesses and professional environments are social, relational environments.
- We cannot assume what feels safe for another person.
- Shift language from *safe space(s)* to *brave space(s)*.

_____

_____

_____

_____

_____

_____

_____

_____

_____

_____

CHAPTER 3

Root, Role, Identity, and Privilege

"Identity is the meeting of who you are, who you believe yourself to be, and who others tell you that you are. It's nuanced, complicated, and hard to define."

–Dr. Yaba Blay

Root and Role

When I'm working with clients 1-on-1, one of the first deep dives we do is what I call *Root*. Root is where we cover everything that feeds into role and identity, which leads into the most impactful part of my work—core values and relationships.

Examining your experience and the environments that influence your identity help shape a deeper understanding of:

- Who you are
- What you believe

- How you interact and behave in the world
- How you might evolve your beliefs
- Where you have opportunities to make an impact
- How you make decisions

You have to clarify the roots of your roles in order to understand and connect to your purpose within each social environment you engage in.

Start by defining your current roles at work, at home, where you volunteer, etc. and how you help others in those roles. Consider the impact your role has on the people in the social environments you occupy, and how you *want* people to experience you. Think about your responsibilities and how fulfilling them impacts those around you.

Once you do this, think about how you do what you do. If you have a process, outline it from start to finish. Think about things you've done in the past that worked well and things you've done that didn't work well. For example, if you have a podcast and you've tried to invite more diverse guests to share their perspective, but few have accepted the invitation, why might that be? Perhaps there's something in your messaging or your previous guests shared harmful rhetoric that led people to decline the invitation. With this example in mind, consider what you want to continue doing and what you want to shift away from. How do you want to use your role and influence? When you evaluate your role, responsibilities, and the processes you follow, you will be better able to discern who you can show up for as well as the areas where you need more development and support.

Connect with people you work and interact with and ask them how they would describe you. You can ask them to offer 3-5 words that encompass how they perceive and experience you. Consider common words, phrases, and themes and compare them alongside your reflections from this section. This is what you will use to help revisit the character of who you are as an individual and how it translates to your role in the social environments you participate in.

Identity and Privilege

When was the last time you really thought about your identity? On the surface, identity can be summed up by your race, gender identity, sexual orientation, socioeconomic status, mental and physical ability, and spiritual or religious practice. These identifiers also determine your social privilege. Being aware of where you have social privilege will help you show up in more supportive ways for those who have less social privilege than you.

For instance, my identity is comprised of multiple intersectional identities being Black, bi-racial, queer, and a woman. On the social scale of white supremacy, I am at a disadvantage for each of these identities since I am not white, male, or heterosexual. However, I have social privilege being that I present as more feminine so I'm less likely to experience discrimination for being queer, unless I'm displaying affection with another woman in public. I also acknowledge that people find me attractive, which apparently makes me less threatening, however, this also exposes me to undesired harassment from cisgender, heterosexual men. In addition, I am relatively financially secure and able-bodied, so I have more freedom and privilege than someone who is disabled and dependent on financial support from other people or state and government institutions.

If we consider another example with a non-disabled, financially secure, white, heterosexual woman, by comparison, she would immediately hold more social privilege than someone like me because of her ethnicity, sexual orientation and potentially her socioeconomic status. Her only disadvantage on the social scale of white supremacy would be that she is a woman.

Alternatively, consider a cisgender, heterosexual, man, who immigrated to the United States from a middle eastern country and practices Islam. He would be more likely to face discrimination for being an immigrant and practicing the Islamic faith compared to a masculine presenting, white, American man who doesn't practice any religion.

It's also important to consider access to safety in relation to social privilege. People who experience even less social privilege, and subsequently less safety than the preceding examples, include people who identify as transgender. Particularly Black, transgender women, who face higher rates of discrimination, violence, and murder because of their identity. Human Rights Campaign, one of the largest and most effective mainstream advocacy organizations in the United States, reported 2021 as the deadliest year on record for transgender and non-binary people. They stated that the majority of people killed were Black or Latinx, transgender women, noting that the stories of victims are often unreported or misreported.

I spoke with Cory Quailes (he/him/them/they) who is a professor and DEI Committee leader at the University of Arizona. Cory shared that it's sometimes easy to take safety for granted as a cisgender man who presents as masculine. He recognizes the privilege he has compared to other people with more intersecting identities. Cory shared a story with me about a friend who is nonbinary and performs as a drag queen. Cory was visiting this friend during a time when they had a scheduled drag performance. The venue was close enough to walk to, but due to fears of discrimination and lack of safety it was decided that Cory's friend shouldn't walk to the venue in drag alone. So Cory and some friends walked with them. Fear of walking alone—especially at night—is something most women can relate to. However, that lack of safety doesn't stop with cisgender women. People in the LGBTQ+ community also share these fears for various reasons—including life-threatening violence. This is one example of why community is so important to people with marginalized identities. Whether or not a person has a supportive community can be the difference between co-creating safety or putting their life at risk.

Kaig Lightner (he/him), Founding Executive Director of Portland Community Football Club (PCFC) and CEO of Quantum Gender, graciously shared his experience related to identity and privilege being a white, transgender person who presents as a cisgender male. Kaig speaks frequently about his experience as a queer, transgender person alongside the importance of inclusion for people in the LGBTQ+ community. He is most known for his work with youth sports and going viral in 2017 after sharing his story with a team he coached at PCFC. Sports has been an integral part of Kaig's life since childhood and it served as an outlet to help him navigate his identity. Growing up, he was bullied and harassed by peers, often asked if he was a boy or a girl because he didn't fit into the gender binary. When we talked about privilege in relation to identity, Kaig shared that he recognizes the amount of privilege he had growing up in a loving, supportive home with family who created space for him to be who he is, without fear of rejection.

> "I always had a safe place to go home to. Things at school might've been really hard. I might've been getting bullied and picked on and teased all the time, but I could go home and feel totally safe, very much seen. It's not to say that there weren't still conflicts, but I wasn't ever, ever, ever getting the message from my family that there was something wrong with me. Whereas the outside world was telling me there was something wrong with me. So that was kind of my foundation that I think is really unique. I think it holds a lot of privilege in and of itself that I had a family that was so supportive of me."

Having a supportive family is important for all human beings. However, people in the LGBTQ+ community (especially transgender people) experience being rejected by their families at higher rates than people who identify as heterosexual. Transgender people also often receive the least amount of care and compassion from society in general, which adds a lot of trauma to their experience. Kaig talked about the day he called his mom to tell her he couldn't keep living in his body the way it was and it was taking a toll on his mental health. He had been on hormones for a year and wanted to have top surgery. His mom was ready to support him in any way possible. The continuous support from Kaig's family helped him work through the challenges that many transgender people experience and he was able to heal through the process. As a result, Kaig doesn't experience trauma triggers or anxiety like many other people do. Not having the same trauma around identity and lived experience as other transgender people is what allows Kaig to share his experience so openly and advocate for LGBTQ+ rights. He recognizes that other people who share a similar identity might not be ready to share their stories, and that's okay.

"When I realized that A) I've got a privilege that a lot of other trans folks don't and B) I have an opportunity to potentially tell a lot of people who think a whole lot of terrible things about trans folks or have a lot of very rooted stereotypes in their mind about the kind of people that we are, that I could show them, 'Well, this is one example of one trans person out in the world

53

who's happy and finding success and, you know, is just living their life, like we all want to.' This started really occurring to me that I had this special gift. And I recognize that it's a gift and I am pretty open about saying such things. Every presentation that I do, I give a very clear disclaimer to everyone that this is something I love. This is something I feel passionate about. I want to be here to tell my story. I want to be here to put myself out in front of all of you. And this is not to be expected of other trans folks and this can be very difficult. So I think that when it comes to the role of leadership, when you find yourself in the position where people are listening to you, you have decisions to make, you have the possibility and the potential power to influence other people's lives—that's a leadership position. And I think the experience that I've had of introspection...that process I've gone through of really digging deep on who the heck am I? How do I wanna be seen in the world? What are the things that are so critical to my sense of wellbeing that they must come true in the way that I present myself to the world? And I think the process of going through transition and literally seeing myself change and finding this person that I am, I think that roots the value system that I hold. I've had that ability to find those value systems. Things like integrity. That's so, so, so critical to me. It is my guiding light. I can talk all day long about inclusion and diversity and all these big buzzwords, but if I turn around and do something in a leadership position that is exclusive or is not in integrity to me, then who am I to stand up there?"

Kaig also explained how he's noticed a major shift in the way he's able to move through the world being a white, cisgender presenting male:

"It never even occurred to me that I would fit into the binary so easily. I do not identify as a man in any way, but externally, I fit into every possible bucket that our society sees as holding privilege and power. When I mention in presentations or things that I do about the interesting experience of being seen as a straight white, people are like, 'What does that mean? What is it? What's the difference? What was it like before? What is it like now?' And for a long time, I had a really hard time answering it because the privilege of white men is so embedded into every nook and cranny of our society in ways that you almost can't even see unless you've experienced something different than that privilege.

A really tangible example that I've started giving to people helps frame it. A few years ago when we were living in a different neighborhood, I'd go out for a run with no problem. And then my partner, who is queer, but presents as everything our society sees as a woman, started going for walks by herself. She'd come back and tell me about cars slowly driving by and men leering at her and honking and doing all this stupid disgusting stuff. And when she told me this, I was enraged. I was like, 'What? How is this possible? How is this possibly happening?' And then it suddenly occurred to me where I was like, 'Oh my God, I can be running or walking in this exact same neighborhood down at the exact same street and have a completely different experience than she does. And just because of how I look, those people don't know that the insides of my body actually look very different from what they're expecting. But everything on the outside looks [like a white male].' And it was that experience that made me recognize this is the white privilege, the social safety net and psychological safety net. That privilege might look a lot different if I was a Black man or a Latino man. That very specific connection of the color of my skin, my gender presentation, and my physicality in the world [allowed me] to take care of myself. I got to go for a run and get my exercise, and my partner comes home and she's just a mess because of her experience being harrassed."

This tangible example from Kaig about recognizing identity and privilege in something seemingly as simple as walking or running in a neighborhood reinforces the reality that women, queer people, and Black and brown people aren't able to move through the world as freely or safely as white men.

Think about your identity and where you have social privilege and how you can use it to support and advocate for people and movements that don't share the same social advantages as you. Then consider the external layers that your identity can support. For example, if you're someone who is always invited to contribute in meetings or projects and you notice someone else who is often spoken over or ignored when they attempt to contribute, use your voice to advocate for that person and create space for them to share. Alternatively, if you notice someone being followed or harassed on the street, do what you can to safely intervene. Your presence and support could benefit the well-being of another person.

The chart below, shared by Tony Nabors (he/him), Founder and Equity Consultant at Racial Equity Insights, provides a breakdown of dominant and marginalized groups and the oppression they experience. This will help put into perspective where you have social privilege.

Dominant Group	Marginalized Group	Oppression
White	People of Color	Racism
Colonizer	Native/Indigenous	Colonialism
Cisgender Men	Women, Transgender, non-binary genderfluid, gender neutral	Sexism
Able-bodied, Able-minded	People with a disability	Ableism
Christian	Other religions or spiritual practices	Christian Hegemony
Heterosexual	Lesbian, Gay, Bi, Queer	Heterosexism
Adult	Youth/Elder	Ageism
Wealthy & Middle class	Poor and working class	Classism
Citizen	Non-citizen	Nationalism
Formally educated	Non-formally educated	Elitism
English speaking	Non-English Speaking, English with an accent or dialect	Linguicism

Your identity is shaped by social environments, connections, and experiences. It's important to pay attention to what inspires, excites, and challenges you so you're aware of how you interact with others in the environments you occupy. Think about how you want people to feel when they interact with you or how you want them to speak about you when you're not in their presence. Your impact on others also has the power to influence how they move through the world, so it is vital to tap into your self-awareness in all areas of your life, beyond your role as a leader.

When you take time to think about your passions, the things you enjoy, how you can support people and movements, and the way your personal experiences influence how you show up as a leader, you will uncover your core values. In Chapter 5: Core Values, Beliefs, and Commitments, you'll learn in depth about connecting to your core values because your core values are the soul of who you are and they can essentially act as a compass to guide you in everything you do. Your core values will support your identity, but before you can solidify them, you need to connect to yourself and what you truly need as an individual in order to show up and embody who you want to be. This is also part of the path to creating a sense of belonging from within, which is vital if you want to create a sense of belonging for other people. When you identify your core values and you intentionally operate through them, everything you do will begin to feel more natural and automatic. Making decisions will be less stressful and you will feel grounded in trusting yourself.

Actionable Reflections:

1. Define your current role(s) and how you help others with your position. How do you *want* people to experience you?

_____

_____

_____

2. How does fulfilling your responsibilities impact those around you?

_____

_____

_____

3. Connect with people you work and interact with and ask them how they would describe you. You can ask them to offer 3-5 words that encompass how they perceive and experience you.

_____

_____

_____

4. What inspires, excites, and challenges you?

_____

_____

_____

5. How do you want people to feel when they interact with you? How do you want people to speak about you when you're not in their presence?

_____

_____

_____

CHAPTER 4

Self-Reflection, Self-Connection, and Belonging

"The most important relationship you have is the one you have with yourself."

—Unknown

Self-Reflection

One of the most important lessons I've learned from this work is that it requires healing and it's far more challenging to create a sense of belonging for others if you haven't learned how to create a sense of belonging within yourself. In order to do this, you need to incorporate healing modalities through self-reflection and self-connection. Developing a healthy, healing relationship with yourself requires being able to clearly identify and communicate what matters to you. When you're clear with yourself first, then you can make the connections you want to make with other people, and you'll find that it's much easier when you know what you need, value, and expect. People who are drawn to you are a reflection of what you put out. In order to connect with people in a genuinely welcoming way, you'll need to clarify what you value and desire in the relationships you participate in, beginning with the relationship you have with yourself.

Think about what you need, value, and expect. Then consider where you can grow and evolve while honoring your needs, values, and expectations. You create patterns and opportunities through the connections and decisions you make so it's important to be aware of how you're showing up for yourself and what you're demonstrating to be acceptable. This also flows into the types of environments you create and the communities you build and participate in. If creating inclusive environments is important to you, how are you demonstrating it?

Be really honest with yourself when you get into self-reflection. What do you really think about yourself and how do those thoughts make you feel? If you find that discomfort arises, don't shut down. Explore it and get curious. Discomfort is an invitation to learn more about yourself. When you're willing to dig into the discomfort you have within yourself, it will help prepare you for working through any discomfort when it comes to engaging with other people and deconstructing any preconceived narratives that may exist about individuals or groups of people. Practicing self-reflection is how we grow and evolve.

Self-Connection and Belonging

In order to self-reflect, you need to be able to connect to yourself on a deeper level. Determining what modalities, or therapeutic practices, feel good to you when it comes to connecting with yourself is the key. When I work with clients in this area, I often share things that have helped me and invite them to take anything that feels good for them. Clients have provided great feedback on the ways some of the modalities I share have helped them. When you're able to connect with yourself at any point, it becomes second nature to give yourself what you need and create your own sense of belonging. Here is a list of modalities that I use for myself and share with clients to practice either on their own or with a licensed therapist or certified practitioner:

- Journaling
- Voice notes
- Meditation
- Breathwork
- Movement
- Mirror work
- Serenade
- Play

I love a good journaling session as do many of my clients. I also acknowledge that not everyone likes to sit down and write. If you're someone who doesn't find journaling appealing, voice notes are a really great alternative. You can speak to a voice recorder and receive the same benefits of journaling without having to write a single word. In fact, it has a lot of benefits! Not only does speaking out loud help process emotions, it also helps you connect to how things feel in your body and where you feel those feelings in your body. When you learn to decipher which parts of your body are activated when you're feeling different emotions, it will help you discern when something is right or wrong for you. This has been a game changer for me, clients, and even friends who have chosen to practice it.

Breathwork and meditation have become the most powerful forms of self-connection for me. If you incorporate these modalities, I encourage exploring them with a certified practitioner if you haven't practiced them before. If breathwork and meditation are things you currently practice or plan to begin practicing, I want to invite you to take some time to learn about the roots of these practices if you haven't already. It's important to honor the origin of any sacred practice you engage in.

I offer movement as a blanket modality. Movement can include any form of exercise, dancing, walking, or stretching. Movement is a great modality for supporting the flow of energy and processing emotions. One of my personal favorite forms of movement to help with energy flow and processing emotions is yoga. Lara Estrada (she/her), yoga instructor and owner of Yoga Bliss, shared with me that her experience has shown her the way movement helps to change how a person feels in a physical, emotional, and energetic capacity.

"Through different yoga poses, or after completing a class, people have shared with me that they have been brought to tears and felt an internal shift. Although I am not an expert in it either, if you study the meridians and chakras (different channels and centers of energy in the body), practices that involve movement can help to improve flow and create more balance. When the physical body moves, the subtle energetic body is moving as well."

Mirror work is another great modality for connecting to self. It feels weird at first, but eventually it can feel as normal as hanging out with a friend. And it should, because the whole idea of mirror work is to spend time with your reflection moving, singing, or talking to yourself and giving yourself positive affirmations just like you would with a friend you care about. I like to approach mirror work by talking to myself like I would talk to a friend in need of some extra love. Sit or stand in front of a mirror and just start talking. You can also record yourself so you have a voice note to refer back to at a later time when you're doing self-reflection work. Author, speaker, creator and spiritualist, Lyvonne Briggs (she/her), describes mirror work as reflection work. She pointed out that African and Indigenous people have been doing reflection work for centuries, beginning with bodies of water when it was simply nature reflecting you back to yourself. Lyvonne shared insight into some of her own practice with mirror work, including dancing in the mirror, getting comfortable in her body, and engaging in what she calls a "radically consensual experience" with herself to connect to her feminine energy. "Regardless of how you identify, you are a blend of both masculine and feminine energy. Many of us were brought up in spaces where you have to be full on masculine. Being feminine has been demonized and belittled." Lyvonne emphasizes the importance of connecting to self and finding joy throughout her work, while encouraging people to get comfortable with their reflection. Mirror work is a powerful modality, especially when combined with other modalities like voice notes, movement, or serenade.

I really enjoy connecting with myself through serenade. This is something you might realize you already do if you like to sing along to music. Think about music that makes you feel empowered or music that is healing to you. This can also include love songs. No joke, in the summer of 2018, I was driving by myself on a mini getaway to the Florida Keys and a string of love songs played through my playlist. I reframed them to myself. Love songs hit really different when you dedicate them to yourself and mean it. Serenading yourself can be a great way to connect to and honor *you*. Personally, Alicia Keys is one of my favorite artists to tune into when I practice this modality.

Play is also a blanket modality as it can be open to interpretation depending on what play means to you. I believe that incorporating play is vital for leaders because with play comes joy, curiosity, and presence, which are all necessary elements to creating belonging.

Practicing various modalities to connect and reflect will help you more easily move through the work of creating belonging within yourself so that you can then create belonging for others. Creating belonging for yourself and others is a journey and it doesn't happen overnight so remember to be patient with yourself while remaining diligent and consistent to your commitment to these forms of wellness.

Inclusive Wellness

Practicing self-reflection and self-connection are forms of wellness. I can't close this chapter out without sharing some additional perspective for you to be mindful of when you take the time to incorporate wellness practices or enter wellness spaces. I spoke with Dr. Portia Jackson Preston (she/her), CEO of Empowered to Exhale, Assistant Professor of Public Health at California State University Fullerton, and TedX Speaker. Dr. Preston specializes in equity-minded wellness, holistic well-being, and sustainable work practices. She pointed out:

> "We tend to think of wellness as something that we do with the abundance of resources or time that we have available. So for example, we might make time to spend with friends, have a leisurely meal, or have a workout... All of this implies that we have the time and resources to do it. Inclusive wellness means that we have to pay attention to the spaces that have traditionally not been accessible for specific

populations, or they are spaces in which they have not been comfortable.

I first really became aware of this even being situated within my own privilege. For example, I could afford to go to a mindfulness retreat, but I might arrive there to find that I'm the only person of color or the only Black woman. And that just added to it, its own filter where I had to really process what the skills that they were teaching me looked like through my own lived experience. I would have loved to be in a space where there were more people like me with whom we could navigate that together. And you know, that really just takes an intentionality in creating the work to be tailored to diverse needs and mobilizing people who represent those audiences to disseminate the knowledge.

When the gatekeepers don't look like you, it takes a lot of internal motivation to override that and continue to pursue your wellness. The second thing that I think of is that wellness is often communicated in a way that is not affordable. Especially if you're already struggling with the basic needs. So if you are struggling to put food on the table or to have shelter, you really don't have time to think about self-care. So I think about how we can expand our definition of wellness. I'm not saying that we have to get rid of the massages and the pedicure and the spa. I do still enjoy those and they have been beneficial for me, but I wanna make sure that when I speak to people about wellness, I'm creating something that is relevant to them. And so for me, that is the sustainable bite size pieces that will help people to breathe in their everyday lives so that they have assessments that they need to do that larger body of thinking about how we can shift and address systems."

Dr. Preston's perspectives on wellness are important here because regardless of the amount of privilege you have, we all need to think about wellness differently, with a more accessible, inclusive lens. This is why I appreciate Dr. Preston's approach to share sustainable bite-sized pieces like a list of modalities to support self-connection and belonging which will ultimately flow into the ways you're able to show up and help create more inclusive spaces. These are things that can be done in small or large amounts of time, even if investing in things like retreats or fitness/wellness programs aren't possible. Dr. Preston also offered her perspective on sharing wellness practices with other people noting:

"Things that have helped me are to really make sure we have more representation, people of diverse backgrounds doing this work and doing it in a way that is relatable and relevant and tangible for people. Sometimes, with the exercises we do, I would have a really hard time telling people in some communities to do a loving kindness exercise. But if I tell them to pay attention to what they might be feeling in their body and I'm patient with them while establishing that connection, we might get to a point where [a loving kindness exercise] makes more sense to them. The same thing happens when I talk about self-compassion or self-care. Sometimes these are not terms that people are comfortable with using, but if we start from a place that is relevant and accessible to them, or has to do with something that they're really invested in, like being able to care for their families, and understanding that caring for themselves is a foundation for that, then they might be able to see an activity such as journaling or meditating as part of getting them to their larger goal. So, when I think about journaling, for example, I would definitely think of prompts that are relevant to a community, but also to take a step back and say, wait a minute, is this something that's feasible and acceptable? If people don't have that practice of writing for pleasure, what is another way to accomplish the same goal?"

Having the ability to reframe perspectives is a necessary skill that will help you move through this work and turn it into an automatic practice. This includes being able to reframe your own perspectives through self-reflection and self-connection. This will help you consider perspectives and experiences of people who will also benefit from your commitment to creating more inclusive spaces.

Actionable Reflections:

1. What modalities will you use to aid in your self-reflection and self-connection?

   _____

   _____

   _____

2. After you choose your modalities, incorporate them into your routine and practice them at least 2-3 times per week.

   _____

   _____

   _____

3. How can you reframe your perspective about wellness practices?

   _____

   _____

   _____

CHAPTER 5

Core Values, Beliefs, and Commitments

"What counts in life is not the mere fact that we have lived. It is what difference we have made to the lives of others that will determine the significance of the life we lead."

—Nelson Mandela

Leadership is a brave choice. As a leader, it's important to know how to communicate what you value in order to draw people in who not only want what you have to offer, but who will feel inspired by the way you show up and lead in your community. I want to invite you to incorporate a daily exercise. You can choose to practice this exercise for a few minutes a day at any point that feels good for you. I recommend doing it in the morning as you're getting ready for your day. Look in the mirror if it's accessible to you and say to yourself out loud: *I am a leader who can inspire people.* Seriously. Say it out loud and repeat it a few times each day.

Tell yourself each day that you are a leader until you don't feel weird saying it. Simply by virtue of being brave enough to take on roles where your guidance is required, putting your work out into the world, and choosing to share your talents, you are a leader. Not everyone is willing to put themselves out there and take chances. This is why it is so important to get rooted in your core values so that you have an internal compass to support you.

Core values are the principles you stand for and the internal mechanism you believe to be vital to your lived experience as well as your brand. You can use your core values to communicate why you make the decisions you do and give deeper insight into what motivates you. Clarifying your core values will help you ensure that you are operating in alignment with your individual character while filtering them through an inclusive lens. It's important to honor your values by evaluating your decisions, connections, and behaviors to ensure that you are showing up in the world in a way that feels true to who you are without sacrificing boundaries or integrity. If you visit BraveLeadershipChoice.com, you will find a link to download my signature Core Values Guide. The exercises in this guide are designed to help bring more clarity and decisiveness into the way you lead.

Now, I realize you may have a different role if you're not a business owner, so for this exercise, I want you to think about yourself as a brand because when you show up in your role at work, no matter what you do for your career or for your clients, *you* are a brand. Even if you've previously gone through the process of defining your core values, I still encourage you to go through the guide and do the exercises because this is an opportunity for you to revisit your values and make sure they're clear. This will also help you determine if your values have evolved at all since you last defined them. In fact, it's beneficial to revisit your values on a regular basis. I recommend checking in with yourself and your team (if you have one) at least once a month to make sure they're being honored; revisit them in-depth at least once a year to determine if they've evolved. Sometimes people ask how their core values could evolve if they're foundational to who they are. Here are two examples of my own core values evolving:

1. One of my core values used to be *relationships* because I care about my relationships with friends, family, and colleagues. Over time, I also recognized that cultivating, participating in, and being supported by community is really important to me. The relationships I have are a big part of that. Because of this, my core value of relationships evolved to *community*. It's still true that my relationships are important to me, and now it's reflected in my value of *community*.

2. *Self-care* has always been a core value, before I even understood what core values were. However, the general idea of *self-care* is commonly summed up to facials and pedicures. While I love a good facial and polished feet, that's not the definition of self-care to

me. I perceive self-care to include things like nourishing myself with good food, remembering to drink enough water, going to therapy, taking time to rest, enriching my mind, distancing myself from people who aren't good for me, and honoring my boundaries. I also wish this for other people so my core value of *self-care* has evolved to *well-being*. I believe it's incredibly important to care for myself and create space for people to care for their own well-being.

When you identify your core values, consider how you perceive your brand through the lens of your values.

1. How are you honoring your core values?
2. How are you representing your core values through your role?
3. Are the decisions you make in alignment with them?
4. If you manage a team, are they clear on the values they're supposed to represent?

It's really important to be clear on this because your values can be used to help you stay aligned in your professional (and social) relationships and interactions. The Core Values Guide is a tool I use with consulting clients during the work we do together. I'm sharing this guide with you as a tool to support you as you work through identifying, defining, and communicating your core values. This will help you get rooted in a foundation to connect all of your decisions to. Think of core values as more than just the principals you or your brand stand for. Think of them as the *soul* of you and your brand.

You can use your core values to communicate why you make the decisions you do as a leader and give deeper insight into what drives you and your brand forward. Your core values are essential to your messaging, and you can use them to share your commitments to your community. By 'community' I'm specifically referencing everyone that connects to you and your brand, whether they're people on your team, professional connections in your network, people following you online, people who buy from you—essentially anyone who supports you. Therefore, it's important to consider how you're communicating your message to them. Your core values can help you communicate your 'why' and serve as a commitment to your community.

Think about why you're attracted to a brand, an organization, or an individual and think about the way you feel when you come across someone or something that you immediately connect with. You might feel excited, happy, or maybe relieved that you found the thing that makes you feel seen. The reason you're pulled towards one person or thing over another is because of your core values. Subconsciously, we all have things we're drawn to, and it's always based on a feeling. When you're clear on the core values for your brand and you incorporate them into the way you operate, you're going to speak directly to the feelings of the people who will be drawn to you. They're going to feel welcomed by you and your brand. They're going to feel seen. When I say 'feel welcomed' I'm specifically talking about the invitation that's inherently embedded in your messaging. This includes the words and phrases you use in your language that communicate to people whether or not they're going to feel comfortable in your community. For example, if you don't use inclusive language or create space for diversity in your stories, people who don't feel represented are going to be more cautious about engaging with your brand. They might feel like it's not for them. Think about how powerful your words are and how important it is to be mindful of the language you use. The people who come across the messaging you create and share are going to recognize how it makes them feel. Remember that your words have power and when you put your message and your work out into the world, you're inherently putting yourself into a leadership role. So be mindful and intentional with your messaging and make sure it's clear and consistent. Being able to tie everything you do back to your core values is the key to formulating clear, consistent messaging.

Once you have your core values defined, you should be sharing them by adding them to your website, talking about them on social media, and reminding people about what your brand represents. When you operate with your core values in mind, you will find that it becomes easier not to question or second-guess yourself before you start a new project or share anything with your community whether it's through social media, a podcast, or your exclusive email list. Your core values should essentially act as a built-in compass for your brand. Operating through the lens of core values makes it much easier to make decisions. I know when people choose to work with me, chances are that it's because they feel a connection to at least a couple of my values, which has made it easier to create more aligned connections. You can create aligned connections through your values too, by using the core values guide offered earlier in this chapter. Ideally, you will choose 3-5 core values to root your brand messaging in. In full transparency, some people feel overwhelmed by the list of words provided in the guide at first because they identify 25 words that feel like values to them. To help with narrowing down your values, I advise you to think about the economy of the words, what they mean to you, how they can be used, and whether or not any of the words from your initial list can be moved under others as sub-values. Additionally, if you did the exercise from Chapter 3: Root, Role, Identity, and Privilege, where you were prompted to ask people to describe you, you can also use common themes from their answers to narrow down your core values.

For instance, if you have empowerment, education, inclusion, and social impact, but you already have four other values listed that you know you don't want to change, which of *these* four words can encompass the rest? Personally, I would choose empowerment because when people have access to education, they're empowered with knowledge that no one can take from them. When inclusion is incorporated, not only do you create a sense of belonging, but you also elevate people from marginalized communities...and that is empowering. It's similar to social impact. When energy and resources are directed to areas and communities in need, it elevates and empowers the people in those communities. When you narrow down your values and you find that you have sub-values, you don't have to hide them from your audience. You can still incorporate and share them in relation to the primary values they fall under and in doing this, you'll be able to stretch out your message and create additional content from it, if you're producing content on a regular basis.

After you choose your values, you'll need to describe why each one is important to you. Be thoughtful. Try to avoid one-sentence answers when you do this exercise. You'll also need to be able to describe how your values are a benefit to your community and the people you work with. For example, trust is one of my core values and it's a benefit to my clients because they often share very personal and sometimes confidential information with me. They need to know that they can trust that I'm not going to take what they share and use it to shame them in any way or use their intellectual property in my own programs. When you do this exercise for each of your values, free write to start, but think about how you would share it with your audience on social media, in blog posts, on a podcast, or any other platform. The reason for this is because I want you to be able to take your core values and turn them into content that can last you weeks or even months. You'll have themes to relate to over a period of time, especially if you want your messaging to drive engagement and connections that result in sales.

To give you an idea, if your values are freedom, empowerment, well-being, community, and trust, you can break them down into weekly or monthly themes and focus your content around each of those values over your chosen period of time. If you have sub-values under your primary values, you can incorporate those into the conversation, but you'll need to do the same exercise to describe why the values are important to you and how they benefit your community and the people you work with. Think about how these things can be related to each part of your brand. Defining, sharing, and talking about your core values is necessary because not only are you letting people know what's important to you as a leader, (remember: we've already established you're a leader by putting your work out into the world) you're also continuously reminding yourself, and anyone representing your brand, of what to pay attention to when you're making decisions and interacting with other people. The idea is for you to get to a place where everything you do can be tied back to at least one of your core values. This includes any decisions you make around hiring people, accepting opportunities, creating offers, or getting involved with other organizations.

One additional thing to note is that your brand's values might differ from your personal values, and that's okay! As long as they aren't drastically different. You don't want to give people the sense that you aren't really who you say you are when you share your brand values. You can also use these exercises to define the core values that are important to you in any relationship because it's very likely that the values you seek in individuals you form relationships with will be more personalized than the values you use in your brand. In fact, I highly recommend you take the time to define your core values for relationships because the relationships you form with people--whether they're personal or professional--will have an effect on how you show up in other areas of your life.

That said, you'll want to make sure the people you connect with feel aligned with who you are not only as a brand leader, but as an individual.

I know when people choose to work with me, it's because they feel a connection to at least one of my core values. I also know it works for people who implement the work we do together because of the messages I receive. One of the best messages I've received was from a client who implemented the core values focused messaging we created together. He shared how he booked a dream client and thought to himself, *"Fuck yeah! Crystal's program works!"* I still have a screenshot of that message saved in my digital praise folder because it's an awesomely direct pick-me-up on the days when imposter syndrome creeps in. And if the profanity here made you do a double-take, then I should let you know that two more of my core values are freedom and empowerment. Within those values, I want to feel free and empowered to express myself unapologetically. This includes occasionally (okay, frequently) swearing to express excitement (or frustration) and I affirm this to be acceptable because my Nana's favorite word was *fuck*, which will always make me laugh when I recall memories of her swearing. Therefore, I also want the people I interact with to feel free and empowered to express themselves with colorful language, especially when they're giving praise.

To be clear, swearing isn't the only reason *freedom* and *empowerment* are two of my core values. I also believe people deserve freedom and autonomy to live their lives and make choices that allow them to be the best version of themselves, without oppression. It's empowering when people are able to operate freely. This is particularly true for people from marginalized communities. Consider Oprah Winfrey as an example. Oprah was born to a poor family in rural Mississippi during Jim Crow. She rose from her humble beginnings to become an influential billionaire, who has inspired millions of people around the world and impacted the lives of many through her programming and philanthropic contributions. Oprah embodies empowerment in ways I have admired since I was a child watching her talk show with my Nana after getting home from school.

Core Beliefs

Once you do all of the work to define your core values, then you can get into your core beliefs. Think about what you believe surrounding topics like human rights, community, education, spirituality, safety, and any other topic you feel to be important to you and your business.

Now because inclusion and empowerment are key components of the work I do with clients in their branding, consider these questions:

1. When you look at your core values and beliefs, how do inclusion and empowerment fit into your message?
2. Can you tie either of them to any of your core values?

When you do this, think about how you can communicate your commitment to inclusion and empowerment in your brand messaging and come up with 3-5 commitments you plan to practice. You don't have to announce these commitments to your community if you don't want to; you really shouldn't have to because if you're actively practicing them, your community will likely be able to recognize it as your message evolves through this work. Take your time with these exercises. Be intentional. Your core values and beliefs are going to be the root of your brand and overall way of being, so it's vital that what you share feels aligned to who you are and the *way* you want to connect with people.

Finally, be patient with yourself. You might not identify your values right away in one sitting and that's okay. This is where intentionality comes in. If it takes a few days or weeks to really hone in on them, there's nothing wrong with that. What's most important is that you feel grounded and represented in the values you choose. If you feel any uncertainty, find someone who is familiar with you and your brand that you can use as a sounding board. Remember: Simply by virtue of choosing to connect to your values, leading with what matters to you, and operating with your values in mind, you can inspire people because not everyone is willing to intentionally operate from their core values out of fear of deviating from the status quo and what's considered 'safe' or 'normal' or 'acceptable.

Actionable Reflections:

1. What are your core values?

   _____

   _____

   _____

2. How are you honoring them?

   _____

   _____

   _____

3. How are you representing your core values through your role?

   _____

   _____

   _____

4. Are the decisions you make in alignment with your core values?

_____

_____

_____

5. If you manage a team, how do you communicate to them the values they're supposed to represent?

_____

_____

_____

CHAPTER 6

Disrupting and Identifying Bias

"We can't become what we need to be by remaining what we are."

–Oprah Winfrey

In this chapter, you will be invited to revisit the modalities you chose in <u>Chapter 4: Self-Reflection, Self-Connection, and Belonging</u> to support you with self-regulation as you engage in the work of disrupting and identifying bias. Doing this will ensure you have what you need to create an effective toolkit for yourself that will help you create a brave space where you're able to tune into your awareness and care for yourself with compassion.

While I am trauma informed—meaning I understand what trauma is and that most people have experienced trauma, and I know how to recognize and reduce harm within my scope—I am not a licensed therapist or social worker. For this reason,

I do recommend working with a therapist or counselor if you need additional mental health support while engaging in this work. One of the main challenges I recognize people experience is an inclination to pull back when they feel internal resistance to new information, particularly around bias. Having modalities to help manage discomfort when it arises is beneficial because it helps create space to process what's coming up so that you can continue to move forward with re-working old, harmful ideas and belief systems. If you are a person who also identifies as someone from one or multiple marginalized communities, this can also help you work through challenging situations where you're either on the receiving end of bias or also trying to help other people do this work. It's equally important to note the reality that even we, as people from marginalized communities, are not without bias. It presents itself within the LGBTQ+ community as well as the Black community, among many others. If we expect people outside of the communities we're a part of to do better, we must live by example.

Before you can implement modalities to help process what comes up, it's necessary to be able to identify what you feel— essentially naming the emotion, noticing where you feel it in your body and the physiological response that accompanies the feeling, and acknowledging how you want to respond. If you have a hard time naming emotions beyond general feelings of happiness, sadness, anger, etc., a quick Google search of the words 'emotions wheel' will produce an array of helpful graphics. Notice I stated how you *want* to respond because the idea is that you don't *react*, but rather become aware and *acknowledge* how you might instinctively react if you didn't have a pause or awareness to filter through. The modalities that resonate with you the most are what I recommend you add to your mental toolkit to help you manage any discomfort that arises when you're engaging in bias work for yourself. I also want to invite you to make note of the other modalities so that you can share them with people you engage with in the event you find yourself in the presence of another person who needs support working through their own biases.

There is an exercise available at BraveLeadershipChoice.com to help you connect to feelings in your body. It's a visualization exercise intended to help you form a connection to feelings in your body and how they affect you. The purpose of this visualization is to help you shape a better understanding of how harmful behavior connected to bias can impact people. If you have been advised by a medical professional not to engage in any sort of meditation or visualization activities or you are currently in a triggered state while processing any sort of trauma, you have the choice to skip this visualization exercise. You know yourself best so please do what's right for you.

Creating A Brave Space

When I think of creating a brave space, I think about an environment where you can be brave enough to be your whole, entire self and also invite others to do the same. This means being able to be honest about who you are and what you believe. This means feeling comfortable enough to share your truth about your lived experiences and how they have informed and shaped your worldview. It's a space where you can get curious about yourself and others without guilt, shame, or judgment and advocate for yourself and others when necessary. A brave space is a place where you can be vulnerable, even if it's just with your own reflection in the mirror.

When a space is created with bravery in mind, this opens up opportunities for you and anyone you share the space with to determine how to be present and find a sense of safety. So how can you create a brave space that you feel comfortable getting curious in and one that inspires others to also show up bravely as their whole selves, especially when it comes to engaging in bias work? You have to understand what you need in order to honor your energy and that requires you to tune into your awareness and get clear on the ways in which you connect with yourself, other people, and the world around you. Your awareness will inform how you respond, so let's get into it.

Tuning in to Your Awareness

Tuning into your awareness is a practice developed through self-reflection and self-connection, where you clarify your values, needs, expectations, beliefs, and behaviors.

Developing this kind of self-awareness helps you determine what modalities feel good to you when you're connecting with yourself and processing information. Engaging in bias work requires a profound understanding of yourself through deep, inner work. One way you can practice self-reflection and connection is by examining experiences and topics that have impacted you both positively and negatively. Perhaps you were impacted by a major life event like landing your dream job or ending a significant relationship. The visualization exercise available at BraveLeadershipChoice.com can also help you with this. When you reflect on your experiences, pay attention to what comes up and how it makes you feel. This will reveal connections to your core values. I've done this exercise multiple times and once, I recalled a friendship that ended. It was emotionally violent, messy, and painful. When I did this exercise, one of the key things that stood out to me was the way we spoke to each other—not just when the friendship ended, but throughout the entire relationship. I recognized there was a lot of sarcasm and snarky remarks disguised as jokes. When I compared that friendship to other relationships where sarcasm and snarky remarks were nonexistent, I realized how harmful the friendship was. I also realized that even though I grew up in environments where sarcasm was acceptable, I don't actually like it being used at mine or anyone else's expense. This reflection helped me solidify compassion as one of my relationship core values. As we covered in Chapter 5: Core Values, Beliefs, and Commitments, connecting with core values is an effective way to engage in this work from a genuine place, while minimizing worry about causing more harm.

When you reflect and connect to your core values, think about how you can honor those values in relation to your needs, expectations, beliefs, and behaviors. Prioritize the modalities that feel the most supportive to you when you're processing information since these are the tools you're going to need to rely on to help you manage any discomfort that arises when working through bias. You can revisit <u>Chapter 4: Self Reflection, Self-Connection, and Belonging</u> for a list of supportive processing modalities. Consider 2-3 modalities that feel most aligned to you that you believe are effective in helping you work through challenging emotions.

1. What are your preferred modalities for processing?
2. Why do you believe they're the most helpful to you?

Once you're clear on the modalities that you want to incorporate or continue practicing, then you can start asking yourself deeper questions as you work to process information related to bias and any discomfort that comes with it. Earlier in this chapter, I shared that before you can implement tools and modalities to help process what comes up, you have to be able to identify what you feel—name the emotion, notice where you feel it in your body and the physiological response that accompanies the feeling, and acknowledge how you want to respond. Now, here are five key questions for you to consider when you're working through anything related to bias that challenges you:

1. How have you handled discomfort in the past and what behaviors did you engage in in response to that discomfort?
2. How would you like to handle discomfort moving forward? What behaviors would you like to let go of and what behaviors would you like to incorporate?
3. Why do you believe the bias being revealed makes you uncomfortable?
4. Where do you believe the bias being revealed comes from?
5. How might the bias and any behavior related to it hinder you from honoring your core values?

Spending time with these questions whenever you're working to address bias can help you tune into your awareness and respond from a place of curiosity. When you do this, you will be providing yourself with the opportunity to practice self-care and compassion.

Self-Care and Compassion

This is worth mentioning again. Any discomfort you feel related to this work is an invitation to get curious and explore why you feel the way that you do. It is not a sign to clam up and disengage. It's an opportunity to learn and grow so that you can evolve as the leader you want to be. As you incorporate these practices, make sure you include self-care and have compassion for yourself and anyone you engage with. It is important to care for your mind, body, and spirit because this is deep, heavy work. And while it is absolutely important to let it all sink in and revisit everything I've shared so you can think about how you want to be as a person, it's equally important to take care of yourself to ensure that you have the energy to keep moving forward because this work is a continuous practice. It's important to learn how to manage your energy so you can keep showing up for the communities that need you as an ally and advocate.

Disrupting and Identifying Bias

Disrupting and identifying bias is the most challenging and necessary step to creating an inclusive consciousness that other people will connect to. It's natural to overanalyze everything you do and find ways to pick your work and your growth apart. While healthy criticism for the sake of evolving is a good thing, it is also a slippery slope. Before you can move forward, you need to be honest with yourself about where you've been and where you are now. This requires unpacking all of the bias and worries you have about your role and organization, your experiences within social environments, and your experiences in and around marginalized communities (non-white, LGBTQ+, disabled, etc.).

Often, when people think of doing bias work in relation to inclusion and belonging, they only focus on bias related to the perception around identity. Bias isn't just about race, gender identity, or sexual orientation. While this is important, if you're truly committed to incorporating inclusive practices and creating belonging, you need to examine where bias presents itself in every facet of your life. Bias shows up in the way you view your business in terms of what you think you're doing well, what you think you can improve, and areas you're not even aware of but other people may notice. One example of bias related to business might include thinking your client or employee onboarding process is seamless, when in reality there are pieces that would hinder people with disabilities, but you're not aware of what they are. Bias also shows up in your community through the people you hire, exchange referrals from, and seek advice from. Literally every element in our lives influences our beliefs, which form our biases. This is why my approach to disrupting and identifying bias covers personal, professional, and community experiences. That said, consider what bias you have in relation to your role and organization, what bias you hold as an individual in relation to people and communities, and what biases are held in the communities and social environments you participate in.

Identifying bias is almost always uncomfortable, however, it is vital to uncover opportunities for growth. Go through this work without judging yourself, as this is an opportunity to examine bias through an objective lens for the sake of acknowledging where harm may have been done so you can be more mindful moving forward.

During a conversation with Monique Melton (she/her), Founder of Shine Bright School: A community dedicated to pursuing Black liberation thru Education. Connection. Action. I asked Monique about her perspective on disrupting and identifying bias. Monique shared that it's quite a process. Since her work is focused more on examining anti-Blackness, Monique invites her students and community to think about and explore the things that are surprising, feel threatening or offensive, and get curious about why. She even poses the question, "What type of default benefit of the doubt do you give white people that you wouldn't give Black people?" Similar to my approach, Monique challenges people to examine the assumptions they're carrying. She says: "Think about decisions you're making and why. With travel, for example, why isn't Africa on your top ten list? What beliefs do you have about Africa?" Monique also reminds people to diversify the sources and creators of the content they're consuming, stating the unfortunate reality that watching films like Harlem Nights, which contains a lot of gun violence, can reinforce the fear that Black people are violent. Monique's perspective invites people to pay attention to the things they feel surprised or judgmental about and explore the ways the content they consume informs how they interact with Black people.

Identifying Bias in Your Role and Organization

You need to be honest with yourself about where you've been and where you are now.

Examine what comes up in terms of what you think you're doing well and what you think you could improve upon in your role. When I'm working with clients on identifying bias, I like to start by asking simple questions to help them open up. We usually begin by identifying what they like about their current role and organization before highlighting anything they dislike. Then we move on to things that can elicit deeper thoughts and emotions. As you consider identifying bias in your role and organization, think about the things you like and dislike as it relates to your experience. Think about things you're proud of, things that excite you, and what you believe you're doing well and how you affirm the things you believe to be going well. Then think about what you're afraid of and what you believe could be improved and why. Consider anything that frustrates you and how you handle it. Think about everything in your role and organization that sparks any emotion—good, bad, or indifferent—and sit with how it makes you feel because those feelings are influencing the bias you have around your role and organization itself. It's important to be able to recognize what comes up for you. Sit with it and step outside of yourself to reflect on it objectively so you can make any needed adjustments. One way to reflect objectively is to imagine you're a journalist whose job is to report the facts of what occurred in the order of what happened.

Identifying bias in your role is a warm up to the deeper work. It's the first step towards getting comfortable with examining things that are usually easy to ignore when you're going about your day-to-day routine. It's also a start towards being honest with yourself because if you can't be honest about the way you view your role and the organization in which you lead, how are you going to be honest with yourself about heavier topics surrounding bias as it relates to inclusion? Bias work can feel heavy. I encourage you to make sure you do what you need to in order to ground yourself before going to the next section.

Identifying Bias Within

Identifying bias within is a commitment that requires you to reflect on experiences that may bring up a lot of discomfort when you reflect on memories where you may have experienced, participated in, or contributed to memories of harmful situations involving people you interacted with or were connected to. Examples of causing harm include:

- Excluding people because they were "different" in some way
- Spiritual, emotional, or experiential bypassing by avoiding or circumventing others reality
- Using racial slurs, sexist or homophobic language
- Talking negatively about someone else's weight, appearance, or disability
- Using microaggressions

Think about how you feel about being involved in conversations regarding human rights, including, but not limited to race, LGBTQ+ issues, women's rights, access for people with disabilities, and support for people with mental health issues. Consider your feelings and comfort level regarding these topics that have historically been sensitive or taboo to talk about. Examine why you feel the way you do. This is an opportunity to be aware of any frustration that arises and how you manage your energy as you work through it. This will also highlight areas where you believe you're doing well and areas where you have room to grow.

Before you can truly support people who are a part of any marginalized community, you have to be willing to be honest with yourself about how you may have impacted others, be it positively or negatively in previous scenarios where bias may have been a factor. Consider what you would want to repeat for those positive scenarios and what you could have done differently in negative scenarios. In addition, think about *why* you're doing this work *now* and what you can do to remain committed because true inclusion work is an on-going practice. If you want people to trust that you're genuinely inclusive, you have to practice inclusion as an individual as well as through your community.

Identifying Bias Within Your Community and Social Environments

When you're genuinely inclusive, you naturally communicate that all people are welcome on a regular basis through your words, actions, behaviors, and connections. Identifying bias within your community requires you to examine the community around your role and organization and your own interactions within it. This includes evaluating your network, your team, and the people closest to you to determine whether there are any patterns of negative bias that you've experienced or absorbed counter to your core values and commitments to inclusion.

Along with considering your responses to positive and negative scenarios, you will also need to think about if and how you could have helped someone in your community be more mindful with their words, behaviors, or actions, and notice what comes up. Even if you were a bystander in a scenario, it is possible that you caused harm by not taking any action while allowing people in your community to perpetuate cycles of violence and abuse.

'Violence' and 'abuse' in this respect are similar to the previous examples I shared of causing harm that include things like spiritual, emotional, or experiential bypassing. For example, using racial slurs, sexist, or homophobic language, talking negatively about someone else's weight, appearance, or disability, or using microaggressions. Additional forms of harm, violence, and abuse include asking for, demanding, or expecting explanations or educational labor from people who are a part of marginalized communities to help you understand your role or connection to their lived experience, rather than doing the work to learn and understand it on your own. Engaging in this behavior is a display of entitlement and privilege reminding people from marginalized communities of their place in the white supremacist social structure. This can also trigger people to relive memories from their lived experience they would prefer not to recall. There are a variety of educators and resources to learn from about the impact of oppression on marginalized individuals, without demanding unpaid educational labor.

The reason these things are categorized under words like 'harm,' 'violence,' and 'abuse' is because there is a power dynamic at play. When a person from one group (traditionally known to be oppressive) uses language, behavior tactics, or any forms of bypassing—including 'jokes' to make another person or group (traditionally known to be oppressed) made to feel as though they are less than (including forms of gaslighting)—this causes the recipient being harmed to question their own worth and reality. This can often result in a visceral internalization that creates real pain in the body. It inflicts trauma.

I rarely share specific stories or examples from my experiences growing up in a white family, in predominantly white, heteronormative communities, because I don't think it would be as productive as the format in which I do share my experience. But understand this: the reason I am so good at the work I do (and I am really damn good) surrounding inclusion, is more often than not because of things I have experienced within my white family and the communities I grew up in. I've had a front row seat to the things that are often overlooked because they're the microcosms that rest within the bedrock of white supremacy. Most people aren't paying attention to them because they're focused on the "bigger" issues. Yet, the reality is the many microcosms that make up the bedrock are what supports the whole violent system. And the violence within the microcosms isn't what you might normally perceive as violence because it's all done with a smile. And as long as you behave according to the expectations set forth for the comfort of whiteness, you can continue to have the privilege of being recognized, included, and supported. But the moment an issue is raised that threatens the comfort of whiteness, your experience can be erased in a single conversation. And *that* is violent.

As you examine bias within your communities, ask yourself if you want to be connected to groups or organizations that perpetuate harm, violence, and abuse or do you want to be a part of mindful environments with people that believe in helping people and communities heal through genuine connection, understanding, and belonging? The reality is that our words, actions, and inactions have more power than we think and so do our connections to people who engage in harming others. Finally, take stock of your connections and the people you share your time and energy with and consider what ways diversity is or isn't present. Think about why that might be and what you can do about it without causing harm or placing labor onto people who are a part of marginalized communities.

Actionable Reflections:

Disrupting and Identifying Bias

1. After reading this chapter, what have you realized about your role and organization, yourself as an individual, your community, and your social environments? Did you recognize any negative bias that you want to change?

   _____

   _____

   _____

2. Explore how you feel about speaking up to someone in your community who has caused or continues to cause harm.

   _____

   _____

   _____

3. How do you feel about distancing yourself from people, groups, or organizations or potentially losing people—even if they've been close to you—if you determine that they aren't ready to receive feedback about their words, behaviors, or actions because they're not ready or willing to do the work themselves?

_____

_____

_____

4. What do you realize about yourself, your business, and your community through the process of disrupting and identifying bias?

_____

_____

_____

CHAPTER 7

Inclusive Communication

"We can use words to uplift and include. We can use our words to fight back against oppression and hate. But we must also channel our words into action."

—Stacey Abrams

The Power of Language

Language is one of the most powerful tools human beings have. The ability to communicate clearly and effectively can leave a lasting impact. Whether you're communicating through behavior, written, verbal, or visual expression, consistency is vital in inclusive communication.

When I host my masterclass centered around inclusive language, one of the warm-up activities I ask participants to do is to think about two memorable things anyone has written, spoken, or expressed in their presence. One being caring, supportive, and compassionate, and the other being harmful, demeaning, or even bypassing. I invite participants to recall how they felt during both of those instances and the contrasting reflections are often similar. On the positive side, people recall feeling happy, appreciated, and validated. On the negative side, people recall feeling sadness, anger, disbelief, and even physical pain in their bodies from the words that were directed towards them. The responses people share aren't surprising considering the limited number of basic human emotions there are when you remove the extending complexities within them. The point of this warm-up exercise is to remind people that language is powerful. It can cause real feelings of disruption and dysregulation in the body and depending on what a person's current life experience is, words can have a significantly positive or negative impact.

Every time we form words, we have an opportunity to make or break someone else's day. This doesn't mean we should feel responsible for everyone's feelings, however, we should still communicate responsibly with mindfulness and compassion. Of course, it can be challenging to predict what language and phrases might negatively impact a person or a group of people. This is why practicing mindful messaging and word replacement skills can aid you in creating messaging that is empowering, inclusive, and affirming.

In this context, I use 'affirming' to describe language that signals to people from specific communities that you will find ways to connect with and support them if and when they engage with you. And this goes deeper than stating Black

Lives Matter or Love is Love. It's continuously communicating what you believe, who is welcome, and the ways in which you are able to support people. Affirming language is consistent and it helps to set up a brave container for people to show up as they are, to co-create their own sense of safety with you, and to engage openly and honestly in the community you create. The skills you need to create mindful messaging are the ability to pause before you act or engage, practice awareness, and have compassion. It's important to remember that things that don't seem like that big of a deal to one community are actually microcosms of much larger issues in other communities. This is also why microaggressions are harmful.

Remember that the role and influence you have comes with a responsibility. Consider the impact you can make and how it requires a significant level of self-awareness. This includes being mindful of the message you put out whether it's verbal, non-verbal, or visual.

Mindful Messaging

Think of 'mindful messaging' as a filter. That's it. It is simply having the ability to filter what you create. And I don't mean 'filter' in a way that what you share is disingenuous to who you actually are. I mean filter what you share through the lens of awareness and compassion for the community or communities you're connecting with. This is why the three top skills I believe you need to practice are:

1. Pause
2. Awareness
3. Compassion

When you pause before you act or engage, you create time and space to sit with everything that either comes your way or comes into your mind. If you're a person who tends to want to react, try making a shift to pause and sit with things a little longer than you normally would. I recommend 72 hours because it can lead to a more thoughtful outcome each time you find yourself in a moment where you would normally react without taking time to think about the potential impact. When the initial burst of energy from an event has time to flow through you, process, and settle, there is a greater opportunity for you to make more measured, rational decisions. If you don't agree, think about a time when you or someone you know have been reactive and whether or not the outcome was dignified or graceful.

When you're creating content, whether it's a social media post, an article, or even an email, sit with it if you can. Rather than share it right away, take a few hours or a few days—even a few weeks if it's available to you, depending on the subject and relevance of the material. Allow yourself time to evaluate and process what you're creating to help ensure that it will make the kind of impact you're intending to make. If you find yourself in a position where you need to respond to a person or a situation, pause and assess everything you have access to in that scenario. Do research if necessary to learn ways you can reduce the potential for harm before responding. Be sure to consider multiple perspectives before responding, whether it's something happening in a comment thread, an email, or a private message.

There is a difference between being reactive and being responsive. Let's consider these definitions from Oxford Languages:

React - to respond with hostility, opposition, or a contrary course of action to.' I interpret this as taking action on something before you've had time to fully process its impact on yourself, other people, and the related environment or relationships.

Respond - to say something in reply. I interpret this as taking time to pause and process what has taken place, how it has impacted you, other people, and the related environment or relationships. Then think about how you want to reflect the existing impact in a way that shifts the focus from the harm caused to the needs of everyone/everything that was negatively impacted.

When you're in a pause mode, consider how you can craft your response so that it aligns with your core values and beliefs. Think about what you want to convey and the variables related to the potential impact it could have. This is where practicing awareness comes in. Potential variables could include people you're writing or speaking to and how their lived experience informs the way they receive what you have to share. This means you need to have at least a general understanding of who you're communicating to/with and what they care about. Practicing awareness begins with you. It's important to be aware of how things impact you and how that impact manifests in your own way of being and how you show up and engage in the world. When you practice self-awareness, you can learn how to create connections within yourself to form your own sense of belonging. When you understand how to connect with yourself, you can more easily communicate your thoughts, feelings, behaviors, and beliefs when you're engaging and connecting with people. I have found this to be beneficial towards building more aligned relationships both personally and professionally. I define success as having a sense of peace from being in alignment. The peace I feel from being in alignment includes finally trusting my intuition, regardless of external opinions on what is right for me, so I can make better, healthier decisions that honor my needs and values.

When it comes to connecting with people through your messaging, you need to be aware of your audience. Consider how well you know the community you're engaging with and how often you make an effort to connect with them. Think about people who are always showing up as your biggest cheerleaders whether they're in your comments, on your email list, tuned into your podcast, or referring and sharing your work. Your messaging is an invitation that connects people to what you value and the community you cultivate.

Being genuinely mindful of the message you're putting out will signal to people that you care about connecting with them as human beings first and you know that all humans desire and deserve to feel honored and valued. When you take a human-focused approach in your messaging, it is crafted with compassion that avoids bypassing the lived experiences of people who hold less privilege.

One form of bypassing that has been prevalent in online business spaces is messaging that tells people they have mindset blocks or need to work harder. This kind of language is harmful because it is irresponsible to assume a person simply has mindset blocks or a lack of work ethic if you're unaware of what their real lived experience entails. They could be doing the best they can alongside dealing with challenging life obstacles that are competing for their energy. This form of messaging is also manipulative when you consider that it plays heavily on pain points people are experiencing. Instead of formulating messaging that solely focuses on putting pressure on mindset blocks or pain points, consider incorporating questions into your messaging or highlighting transformations people have experienced from working with you, then extend an invitation. Invitations over manipulation, always. Another beautiful focal point to use in selling is one shared by Paige Ray (she/her), Founder and Creative Director at Paige Ray Creative. Paige shares:

"Focus on the dream and the transformation. I like to use something I call the front porch test. I ask my clients to imagine they're in their golden years, sitting on the front porch. Then I ask them what they imagine when they think back on their life. If they did all-the-things and went for what excited them, what would their life look like?"

Paige also clarifies the reality that we can't eliminate talking about pain points in our messaging, but there is an ethical way to do it:

"We wanna talk about the transformation and we wanna lead with that because it's the most important thing. But transformed from what? What is that state we have to identify for people to let them know how we can support them and help their transformation? We have to be able to speak to where they are now by letting them know we understand how they might be feeling because we've helped other people in their position get to where they wanted to be. That requires talking about their pain points, though I think we could rename *pain points*.

What is unethical is making up pain points with messaging that tells people something is wrong with them and manipulating them into buying a product or service they don't need by being pushy and ignoring their '*no*,' or lying about what you can actually do for people."

An elevated invitation in your messaging also considers people with disabilities and any accessibility needs they might have since they will be experiencing the world differently compared to someone who holds more privilege than they do. This includes having alt text for images and closed captioning or transcripts available for videos and audio as well as podcasts.

Victoria Alexander (she/her), an equity and justice educator and PhD student at the University of Maryland, shared on her TikTok account (@victoriaalxndr) that we also need to be mindful of people who use screen readers by spelling things out as they are, rather than using the letter 'x' in place of words like woman or folks. The screen readers may not be able to accurately read the text if it's spelled with an 'x.' Being aware of nuances like this and making adjustments to support people who are a part of disabled communities makes a difference. Accessibility is an area I'm continuing to learn more about and have been working to improve. This is why I refer to Erin Perkins (she/her), Founder and CEO of Mabley Q. Erin, who is an expert in accessibility education, shared her perspective on what leaders need to consider in relation to accessibility for people with disabilities:

> "People in leadership positions take diversity at its face and mainly focus on race, ethnicity, and gender, but fail to consider disability inclusion. If you're committed to closing the disability inclusion gap at your company, here are four strategies you can utilize:

1. Identify and change processes that support unconscious bias. Look beyond people's disabilities when considering them for a position. Their strengths may surprise you.

2. Help your team understand the challenges people with disabilities face and contribute to solutions. Everyone can contribute their best if they are educated about disabilities, accessibility, and inclusion.

3. Strengthen the hiring pipeline by engaging with community groups. People with disabilities may be hesitant to apply for positions with companies that do not present themselves as accessible and inclusive.

4. Create a mutually supportive community. Empower employees (disabled and able-bodied) by providing education and training so that they're all able to achieve success."

Every action–and inaction–sends a message. These strategies shared by Erin are forms of actionable messaging. When you begin formulating your messaging that will serve as your invitation, be mindful of the actions you take and pay attention to the words and phrases you're using both in person and online. Making small shifts like stating your pronouns and asking people for theirs, rather than assuming someone's gender identity, can go a long way. Just because a person presents as masculine or feminine doesn't mean they identify one way or the other. Using non-gendered language is a safe way to go and it's empowering for people who don't identify with the gender binary. I like to say 'y'all,' or 'peeps,' and some people like 'folks,' in place of 'hey ladies' or 'hey guys.' There are options and this is where word replacement comes into play.

Word Replacement

Word replacement is probably one of the most challenging parts of this work because it requires us to catch ourselves while forming communication that has often been automatic. Think about language that is a part of modern communication that has been predominantly socially acceptable, like the phrase 'ladies and gentlemen,' for example. Engaging in word replacement is an exercise for your brain and an opportunity to be intentional about the way you communicate. I recommend practicing this in your content writing first and working it into real-time conversations with the pause filter I shared earlier in this chapter.

When you incorporate word replacement, try to avoid using behaviors as adjectives to describe people or things. One of the most common words people tend to use to describe people or things is the word "crazy" and this can actually be harmful to people who identify with having real mental illness. Replacement words could include 'bananas' or 'wild.' TBD on whether or not those will need to be replaced in the future as our collective understanding of culture and language evolve. Another mindful practice shared by my friend and NYC resident, Leah Weinberg is to "Reconsider labeling people as their circumstances, but rather in their circumstances. Instead of calling someone a homeless person, reframe it to a person experiencing homelessness."

It's also important to avoid using labels or self-identifiers to describe people without their consent. For example, calling or describing someone as "gay." If they are gay, it's not okay to out them without their consent. If they aren't gay and especially if you know this, the description can come across as an insult to people who are a part of the LGBTQ+ community and this perpetuates more harm. It's important to avoid sharing personal identifiers without someone's consent. Be mindful not to disclose someone's sexual orientation, gender identity (if they've shared a personal identifier with you), mental illness, or disability unless they've shared that you can do so. Always make sure to ask for consent before disclosing things that people share with you.

Finally, avoid using ableist or derogatory language. Some examples of replacement language include saying things like: *Did you check out that latest podcast episode?* Rather than: *Did you listen to or hear that latest podcast episode?* Or *Have you noticed the latest updates to Instagram?* Rather than: *Have you seen the latest updates to Instagram?* These are small shifts in language that demonstrate deep mindfulness about the potential lived experiences of other people. I invite you to take some time to do more research on inclusive language and you can do this simply by typing 'inclusive language' into your search engine. A range of resources will come up for you. Remember that these are some suggestions and you can choose what feels appropriate to consider depending on the community you're speaking to.

A final reminder regarding language and mindful messaging is that these are recommendations and it is important to consider the nuances that come with communication. If you are aware of your audience and they are familiar with the way you communicate, some of these suggestions may not apply to you, however, it is still beneficial to use them as a filter when crafting your messaging.

Visuals and Ethical Representation

When you think about incorporating visuals for your brand or organization, they should communicate what you do, show techniques, reflect core values, and invite your community. When I say 'invite your community,' what I mean is to create imagery around things that would draw your community in, in a way that is relevant and also speaks to their emotions. Any visuals you have should be an invitation for your community to take a peek inside what you do and how it can benefit them.

It's also important to make sure your community feels welcome. When you're incorporating inclusive visuals, make sure your brand is a true representation of the people you're inviting in and make sure it's consistent. Please do not use people in brand photos who do not actually identify with the audience you are targeting. For example, do not use models who aren't part of the LGBTQ+ community to represent the LGBTQ+ community or people who aren't disabled to represent people with disabilities. It's also important to avoid tokenizing people, stereotyping, and engaging in cultural appropriation. As I wrote in the <u>Why This Work Matters</u> section at the beginning of this book, incorporating behaviors, language, and practices intended to honor the humanity of marginalized people shouldn't be trendy. Additionally, it's important to remember that people aren't props.

Actionable Reflections:

When it comes to connecting with people through your messaging, you need to be aware of your audience.

1. How well do you know the community you're reaching out to and inviting in with your message?

   _____

   _____

   _____

2. How often do you really engage with people in your community?

   _____

   _____

   _____

3. Who are the ones that are always showing up as your biggest cheerleaders?

   _____

   _____

   _____

4. What do you know about the people in your community or the people you want to invite in, and what's important to them?

_____

_____

_____

There is a difference between being reactive and being responsive.
When you're in a pause mode, ask yourself:

1. How is this in alignment with my core values and overall message?

_____

_____

_____

2. What am I hoping to convey?

_____

_____

_____

3. How could this impact people?

_____

_____

_____

Language to incorporate...
- Pronouns
- Human-focused adjectives (Example: Using words to describe someone's personality, rather than solely focusing on their appearance.)
- Consent-based communication (Example: Asking for consent before disclosing other people's sexual orientation, sexual identity, mental illness, disability, etc.)
- Inclusive language

Language to let go of...
- Gendered language
- Using behaviors as adjectives (Example: Describing people or things as "crazy")
- Using labels or self-identifiers to describe people without their consent. (Example: Calling a person "gay")
- Ableist or derogatory language

Instead of this:	Try this:
crazy	bananas, wild
looks like	represents, reminds
listen to	tune in, check out
see	notice
hear or heard	aware
blind spot	unaware
ladies or gentlemen	folks, peeps, everyone, y'all
stand up for/to	advocate for

Visuals and Ethical Representation:

- Visuals should communicate what you do, show techniques, reflect core values, and invite your community.
- Do not use people in brand photos who do not actually identify with the community they're intended to represent.
- Avoid tokenizing people, stereotyping, and engaging in cultural appropriation.
- Remember: People aren't props.

CHAPTER 8

Embody and Inspire

"You have to act as if it were possible to radically transform the world. And you have to do it all the time."

—Angela Davis

Brave leadership requires you to put yourself in vulnerable positions where you may be the first to make a decision that disrupts the status quo. You might make mistakes when people are expecting you to know what to do at every moment. As a leader, you are taking on the responsibility of influence. This is why it is vital to consider how your way of being impacts other people. This is the part where you will spend more time thinking about how you want to use your influence, traits you currently embody, and any traits you want to incorporate once you've created a sense of belonging from within. Not everyone is willing, ready, or capable of taking on the responsibility of leadership in this way. This is why it's a brave choice.

Connecting to the way you show up and experience the world and the way others experience *you* is necessary when creating awareness around your way of being. Your *way of being* is a culmination of the language you use, the thoughts and emotions you experience, the physiological reactions that take place in your body, and how all of these things translate to your behavior. Your way of being should make people feel welcome as it reflects the core values, beliefs, and commitments you hold for yourself and share with the world. Your way of being will serve as an invitation to the people and organizations that are drawn to you. It will determine the energy you attract as well as the type of community that forms around you as an individual.

When you consider inclusion, make sure your way of being allows space for tuning in to what people share. Inclusion is a daily practice and it requires being open to information that may be new to you. When you're met with new information, pay attention to how you receive, process, and react to it. Then seek ways to understand and integrate the information into your interactions when appropriate. Be sure to do further research on topics when new information is presented to you. It is not fair or appropriate to expect people who are bringing new information to you to educate you entirely on a topic. This is especially true if the people sharing the information are part of a marginalized community, unless they've been hired to guide you. It's also important to avoid tokenizing people, stereotyping, and engaging in cultural appropriation.

Responsibilities of Leadership

Being a leader comes with a lot of perks and even more responsibility. One of the things I've learned from working with leaders to help them incorporate inclusive practices is that balancing the perks and responsibilities of influence are crucial. We live in a time where social currency has led us to platforms that allow us to reach people with internet access anywhere in the world. This is equally amazing and scary. It can be easy to get caught up in focusing on the benefits of having influence and forget about the depth of responsibility that comes with having access to these platforms. It's important to remember the power that comes with influence. It doesn't matter if you have a community of 100 people or tens of thousands. Regardless of the size of the community you reach, you have a responsibility to consider the impact you can make and this requires a significant level of self-awareness.

Self-awareness, in this context, is all-encompassing, including being mindful not to prioritize intention over impact. On the most basic level, 'intent' boils down to 'purpose.' When we say or do things, there is usually an intended purpose. We want to communicate or execute something that we deem necessary. Where intent gets lost is when its impact has a negative effect. 'Impact,' when negative, lands with force. It can be jarring and dysregulating. So often, the phrase "that wasn't my intention" is spoken when a person is made aware of harm they caused. And it is my belief that this phrase is usually employed to try and reduce the impact that's occurred. This is actually harmful because the focus is shifted from the *actual* impact (reality) to the *imagined* intent, often putting the person who was harmed in a position of having to comfort and reassure the ones who negatively impacted them. This can deepen the impact and reinforce the harm, creating a lack of safety and support for the person who actually needs it. Rather than rely on 'intent' as a source of protection from accountability, allow the focus to be on *acknowledging* and *understanding* how the actual impact landed and work to repair and grow from there. Think about how you actually want to impact people, how you can be more mindful in your communication and interactions, and where you have power and influence to help other people consider these thoughts for themselves. Remember that prioritizing 'intent' over 'impact' is an imagined reality.

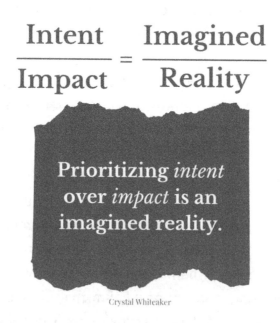

$$\frac{\text{Intent}}{\text{Impact}} = \frac{\text{Imagined}}{\text{Reality}}$$

Prioritizing *intent* over *impact* is an imagined reality.

Crystal Whiteaker

As a self-aware leader, you are aware of the advantages and privileges you have and the influence you have to make an impact, both positive and negative. You understand yourself and how you receive, process, and respond to challenges and feedback because you know what your strengths are and where there is room for growth. You can articulate genuinely what you value and why inclusive leadership matters. On the most basic levels, you are aware of your emotions and behaviors when you're under pressure, tired, excited, or in a creative flow. When you lead responsibly, from a place of awareness and acknowledge the potential impact you can have, the benefits of embodying inclusive, inspiring leadership practices will naturally flow to you. Benefits include building aligned relationships that lead to a more connected community. This will create space for:

- Inspiring collaborations
- Working with clients you're excited about
- Doing what lights you up
- Opportunities your younger self would be in awe of
- A reputation that positively precedes you

These benefits won't appear simply because you do everything "right" all the time, but because you show up honestly and fully in your humanity. This way of being sets an example and creates permission for other people to do the same. This is ultimately about making an impact in ways that are meaningful and influential so that you can cultivate the type of community, support, and wealth (in all forms) that you actually want to have in your life.

Traits of Inclusive, Inspiring Leaders

Inclusive, inspiring leaders are mindful that we all have different lived experiences and are at the very least trauma aware, though ideally they're trauma informed. Being trauma aware means you're aware that most people have experienced some form of trauma and you're aware that you need to be mindful in your interactions with people. Being trauma informed means you have enough knowledge and awareness to hold space for people who have experienced trauma and that you can honor their lived experience without bypassing or minimizing their reality.

Some examples of minimizing someone's reality include phrases like:

- *"It's not that bad."*
- *"It could be worse."*
- *"You're so strong."*
- *"It's just a joke."*
- *"Get over it."*
- *"It's not that big of a deal."*

Being mindful in this way matters because all of us have been or will come into contact with a person who has experienced trauma, and you need to practice mindfulness and compassion in each of your interactions. In addition to this, understanding and practicing consent is also important. You may find yourself in a situation where people share personal or privileged information with you and it's vital that what they share is honored. Be mindful not to press people or coerce them out of their comfort zone too quickly. Believe that people know at least enough about themselves that if their initial response to an invitation or an offer is 'no,' they're honoring what they know about themselves. This doesn't mean that they can't change their mind in the future. However, trying to talk someone into something without allowing them time to process, or pressing on their pain or vulnerability to encourage a sale, is the opposite of trauma informed. And depending on an individual's current situation or even their relationship with money, you run the risk of triggering and dysregulating them and that's not a great way to enter a relationship.

People respect leaders who demonstrate respect for other people and varied ways of thinking. When you engage in conversations with people who think and live differently than you do without judging or shaming them and honoring who they are as a human beings, it's an opportunity to expand your mind and knowledge base in a way that will allow space for diverse ideas and lived experiences where all beliefs and realities can be true, even if they're not your own. By doing this, you'll gain a better understanding of how to communicate across broad spectrums with empathy and compassion. And if someone brings something to your attention that's harmful, ideally, you will lead by example and take accountability when necessary. When you operate in this way and exercise these traits with mindful intention, it should be genuine and honest to who you are and the leadership style you want to embody. When you embody a genuinely inclusive leadership style, you're positioning yourself to help shape a better future for the human collective.

When I think of inspiring leaders who are helping to shape a better future, of course I think about obvious, well-known people, like Oprah Winfrey (Can you tell she's one of my idols?), Barack Obama, Angela Davis, and Brene Brown. I also think of people who aren't as well-known, like Rachel Ricketts, Jordan Maney, Kirsten Ott-Palladino, David Ryan Castro-Harris, Nicole Cardoza, and the generous contributors and educators highlighted throughout this book. There are also plenty of inspiring leaders I follow on social media who are doing incredible things. And let's not forget teachers and local leaders in our communities. Inspiring leaders are all around us. They don't have to be famous to be acknowledged for the work they do to help shape better environments for people.

Creating Belonging from Within

In <u>Chapter 4: Self-Reflection, Self-Connection, and Belonging,</u> I established that we cannot truly create a sense of belonging for other people if we don't know how to create a sense of belonging for ourselves. If you need to, revisit the fourth chapter for a refresh on self-reflection and self-connection before going any further.

One of the most common things people share with me when they engage in this work is that they're worried about saying or doing the wrong thing. This fear is often rooted in insecurities about who they believe themselves to be and how they're perceived. When this concern is shared, I remind people that we all make mistakes and that they will probably make mistakes in the future because it's part of being human. It's how you handle those mistakes that actually matters. If this is a fear that you recognize within yourself, I want to invite you to consider this: Rather than focusing on the fear of getting it wrong, redirect that energy towards connecting to and tuning into what's going on in the community around you, and do your best to honor what people are sharing. Then take time to reflect on whether you're potentially contributing to harm and ways you might be able to be of better support. And if someone brings something to your attention that is harmful, be mindful not to prioritize intent over impact.

Creating space to connect to who you truly are will help you better understand how to create an inclusive community for others. This not only includes identifying and examining biases that you have about other people, ideals, and the world in general, but also biases that you have about yourself because your opinions of yourself influence what you believe about the world, ideals, and other people. It also means being clear on what your core values and beliefs are and operating

131

from them. When you do this, it will open doors–literally and figuratively–that can help you evolve into who you want to be and how you want to lead. By creating belonging from within, you will be able to focus more on your purpose and this comes full circle since your purpose helps create belonging for who you are...and there is so much possibility in that. Imagine leading from a place where you feel so grounded in who you are and how you can serve your community that you're able to inspire others to embrace inclusive leadership practices as well. Once you create belonging within yourself, then you can help create it for others. Detach from being recognized as an inclusive person and focus on the journey within the process. Be present for the growth and discovery within yourself and what you'll learn about your community. Remember that this isn't about checking boxes. It's a continuous, evolving practice.

Actionable Reflections:

Prioritizing 'intent' over 'impact' is an imagined reality.

To recap...inclusive, inspiring leaders:

- Are mindful that we all have different lived experiences
- Are trauma-informed
- Honor consent
- Demonstrate respect
- Understand how to communicate effectively with empathy and compassion
- Lead by example and take accountability
- Embody a genuinely inclusive leadership style

Questions for reflection:

1. How do you want to use your influence?

   _____

   _____

   _____

2. What traits do you currently embody?

_____

_____

_____

3. What traits would you like to incorporate?

_____

_____

_____

CHAPTER 9

Building Aligned Relationships

"Choose people who lift you up. Find people who will make you better."

−Michelle Obama

Being an individual in any role gives you at least a certain amount of influence. Being a *leader* within communities and organizations is challenging and it's important to have many forms of support. Aligned relationships consist of people who can:

- Advise you
- Listen to you
- Challenge you
- Encourage you
- Help you evolve
- Advocate for you
- Collaborate with you
- Remind you of your purpose

I believe it's important to clarify what 'aligned relationships' means in this context. Building aligned relationships does not mean that you solely seek to connect with people who think exactly the way you do. There needs to be space for diverse thinking that leads to curious, considerate, compassionate conversations.

Think about where you are in your role right now. Think about people who have been a part of your journey to help you get to where you are. When you think about people you're connected to, consider where they fit into your community. Communities are made up of various types of people who usually share at least some similar values and belief systems. Understanding this will better help you connect to people on a more human level so that you can learn to connect with one another in consideration of your individual lived experiences all while creating space for people to come together as a collective. When you think about people in your community connecting to your core values, consider your past and existing connections. Think about people you enjoyed being connected to and people you didn't enjoy interacting with. Consider the things you appreciated and didn't appreciate about current and past connections and interactions. When you reflect on your relationships, consider whether or not there was diversity among the people who came to mind. And if there wasn't, take some time to explore why that might be and determine if you can identify any bias as you think through it. As you process these reflections, weigh them against your personal/brand core values as well as your relationship core values that you defined in <u>Chapter 5: Core Values, Beliefs, and Commitments</u>. Remember that your relationship core values might be more particular than the core values you've defined for your personal/brand, so make sure you're clear on what your core values are in both your personal and professional relationships.

To give you an example, imagine that your personal/brand core values are freedom, empowerment, self-care, community, and trust. People you connect with might identify with some or all of those things, but it doesn't exactly outline what you expect to give or receive from the relationships you engage in, so perhaps your relationship core values might be: compassion, patience, understanding, communication, connection, and trust.

When you know what you need and expect from your relationships, you will pay closer attention to the connections you're making to ensure those values are being honored—just like you would with the core values you have for your brand. Be mindful of how you're spending your time and who you share it with. Consider how the relationships you have nourish you. Making connections is networking, and networking is a lot like dating. If you don't vibe with a person or a brand, that's okay. You don't have to keep seeing each other. Don't sacrifice your values in pursuit of shiny connections that aren't going to nourish or support you. When you're clear on your relationship core values and you continuously check in with yourself to make sure they're being honored, it will become easier to connect with people who are more aligned and able to provide value to your community. There are so many benefits in building aligned relationships, especially if diversity, equity, and inclusion is something you care deeply about.

If you've been working on incorporating more inclusive practices and you've felt like the relationships you had with people before you started incorporating inclusive practices changed after you started sharing your perspective or showing your commitment to the work, know that you are not alone. It can feel frustrating trying to explain yourself to people who have always been "your people" when it seems like you're suddenly speaking two completely different languages. This is why forming connections with people who understand why you're engaging in this work will help you lead to building more aligned relationships. Find people you can collaborate with, bounce ideas off of, get support from, or just talk to when you have a tough day because these are the people who will support you the most. When you connect with people who feel aligned, you will experience a deeper sense of understanding that can lend to developing aligned partnerships and collaborations and stronger personal and professional relationships.

Not everyone will be ready to take the journey exactly when you do, however, leaving the lines of communication open allows space for people to learn from your experience if they choose to. I don't recommend cutting people out if you can avoid it. Instead, create distance to protect your well-being. This way, if people decide they want to reconnect and learn later on, they have someone who has already done the work to talk to. Having support through this work is necessary because none of us can do it alone. Always consider how you can help one another when you're meeting and connecting with people because you never know who could lead to great collaborations and valuable relationships, so make sure you're aware of your magic.

Practice Your Magic

Some people call it your "you-ness," others refer to it as a zone of genius, and I have a friend who calls it your special sauce. I call it magic. Your magic is the invisible energy that attracts and repels people. And unless you're really in tune with yourself, your values, and your magic, you might find yourself going in circles trying to figure out why you're having such a hard time connecting with people you *think* you want to connect with, when in reality, you might not be aligned with each other at all. How many times have you tried making connections with people only to find out you didn't vibe at all and it caused you more stress or uncertainty than anything else? I have been there and it's honestly because I wasn't in tune with my relationship values or my individual magic. I was trying to fit in to attract relationships that ultimately weren't aligned. A key component of identifying your magic requires tapping into the work of self-reflection and self-connection from Chapter 4.

It's important to tune into yourself and understand what energy you're holding on to because whether you realize it or not, you're projecting that energy out into the world. Identifying what lights you up and makes you want to engage is a key to identifying your magic and it feeds into what you do and how you show up. Pay attention to what people say about their experiences with you, too. They may be recognizing things you haven't even acknowledged yet. When you know what you value in relationships and how your magic thrives, you can use it to connect with people and form lasting, beneficial, aligned relationships. When you actively practice your magic through a self-aware lens, you will notice patterns when you apply hindsight.

When I worked in corporate, I had a coworker (my work bestie at the time) who was going through a tough time, so I invited her to spend the weekend with me. I didn't think I was doing anything extraordinary. All we did was hang out, talk, eat food, go hiking, and walk on the beach. After those two days, we went about our lives and routines as usual. Eventually, we both took different paths professionally, but we always kept in touch, even though we didn't see each other for a few years. Then, in the summer of 2021, we were able to see each other and it was like no time had passed. She told me how much that weekend we spent together helped her get through her rough patch. She shared how healing it was and told me that she loved the path I took professionally. She believed I was a healer and had a way of connecting to people to help them connect to themselves and see their value as well as the value of others. I was so surprised when she shared this with me! However, it was also an ah-ha! moment. This work of guiding people through the process of becoming aware, disrupting bias, and getting clear on values to incorporate inclusive practices requires being open to connection and healing. What this person shared with me was also in alignment with what my clients have shared with me; clearly my former work bestie recognized my magic before I did.

When you think about your magic in practice, I want you to consider the people you enjoyed sharing time with. Recall the people and moments where you have made an impact. Pay attention to what people tell you when they say you've positively impacted them and determine what about those interactions came naturally to you. Think about a time when you met someone or a group of people you easily connected with—those whom you've enjoyed working alongside, collaborating, or speaking with. Think about what you were doing and how it made you feel. Consider the environment where you had this experience and what you can do to cultivate more of that going forward.

The energy you generate is contagious so the connections you make should feel complimentary to who you are, based on the vibe and space where you operate best and feel the most authentic. When you identify your magic and define your relationship core values, this is where you will begin to connect with your natural energy. Your natural energy is the vibe and space where you operate at an optimum level. Your natural energy also works with your magic to attract and repel people. The less energy you have to exert trying to convince people to acknowledge and support you, the more energy you'll have for the people who want to be in connection with you simply because they're attracted to what you're putting out into the world. This is especially true if you're cultivating an inclusive community.

When you think about people who should feel 'complimentary' to who you are, that doesn't necessarily mean 'just like you.' Not every aligned relationship is going to be someone you want to be best friends with because the reality is that you can connect with people on a professional level and communicate and work really well together, but you might never spend time together beyond a professional capacity, and that's okay. The goal is to tune into yourself and your energy so you can build more genuine, aligned relationships that will help you thrive and support your goal of creating inclusive environments.

When connecting with people, you need to know your story because this is what will help you connect with people who want to be connected to you, support you, and collaborate with you. Get clear on how you want to talk about yourself, what you believe, and what you do, and be ready to confidently share it with people. Be sure to include causes or movements you support and how your story honors your values. These are the things that are going to help you connect with people and create aligned connections.

Seek Inclusive Connections

Once you've connected to yourself, identified your magic, determined what core values need to be met in relationships, gotten in touch with your natural energy, and practiced sharing your story, you should also be seeking inclusive connections that are in alignment with the type of community you want to be a part of. Don't be afraid to reach out and put yourself out there. There are people who want to connect with you and be included in what you're creating. Search for events happening in your area that you can attend and reach out to people and communities that you resonate with. Introduce yourself, engage, and share your story. Relationships grow from genuinely aligned connections. If there is a person or brand you've been wanting to connect with, reach out to them and invite them to have a conversation. The worst thing they can tell you is 'no' and 'no' is not a bad word—it's a motivational word that should encourage you to keep going after the 'yes.'

Nourish Your Relationships

When you're connecting with people and forming relationships, you need to nourish them by engaging, checking in, and asking questions. Consider whether or not you have things in common and how you can help one another. Be mindful of how you can be supportive in the connections you develop, especially if you're a person who holds more privilege in the relationship. Relationships should not be one-sided! If one of you is always giving, but the other doesn't contribute much, it's okay to ask the hard questions around whether the relationship is actually aligned. Check in with how you feel in regards to the relationships you have and remember that the relationships you form do not all have to result in clients, especially if they're nourishing to your spirit.

To share a personal example of relationships that nourish the spirit: There is an incredible group of women I've been connected with since the beginning of 2020. At the beginning of the pandemic, one of them sent out an email to me and several other business owners to ask if any of us would be up for a video chat just to talk. It turned into a supportive weekly video chat and since then, we have helped each other with so much more than business. We've talked about life, social issues, goals, things we're planning and hoping for. We cultivated a necessary community among ourselves that all of us needed. The encouragement and support we've shared is immensely beneficial because we've made each other feel valued and heard. That good energy has poured into my work and I'm able to pour it into the interactions I have with my clients and collaborative partners. That kind of nourishment is a huge benefit!

It is also important to note that nourishing relationships also means honoring boundaries. This is vital because boundaries and inclusion go hand-in-hand when it comes to relationships, particularly when you're engaging in relationships with people who don't identify with your lived experiences. Honoring boundaries requires having honest conversations with yourself and people close to you to make sure you know what you need to take care of you, first, because the most important relationship you can have is the one you have with yourself. You need to know what you're willing and able to do or accept. You need to know how much you're willing and able to give. You need to know what you need to maintain an optimal energy level when you're engaging with people. This means recognizing when you think your boundaries are being pushed and examining how you feel as well as how you react/respond. It's okay to say 'no.' Remember, your 'no' is a motivational word for other people to continue seeking a 'yes' from someone more aligned to their mission. Check in with yourself regularly and speak up when something doesn't feel right.

Let's say you believe in giving back to communities by donating resources like your time, knowledge, or money. Imagine you're presented with an opportunity to contribute to a community through an organization that seems to have an aligned mission. Let's also say you learn that the organization is profiting from the community they're supporting, while benefiting from resources donated by contributors. If you determine that donating resources to a for-profit organization isn't aligned, then honor that and don't be afraid to negotiate. I recommend asking questions and having guidelines around what you're comfortable giving while remaining in integrity with your boundaries. What I mean by this is that if we don't operate in alignment with our values, our boundaries are more likely to get pushed.

I've had to create a policy in my business to ensure the invitations I receive to be a speaker or lead facilitator —that I say 'yes' to—align with my values and expectations. Countless times, I've been invited to talk about inclusion for 'exposure' or an 'energy exchange,' and I've respectfully countered with my speaking fee or declined. Particularly in scenarios where the invitations came from white women I didn't have existing relationships with who wanted to promote inclusivity. In these scenarios, I found myself in the position of explaining why it wasn't appropriate to invite a person of color to talk about inclusion for free when people were paying to be a part of their communities. I have often received surprised looks while pointing out how these invitations perpetuated the history of marginalized people being expected to provide free labor to non-marginalized (usually white) people. These interactions also reinforced how important DEIB work is and that marginalized people need to be paid for it.

Someone said to me once, "You can't make demands until you're in demand." I disagree with this statement because it leaves room for people to be taken advantage of. I know because I've both witnessed and experienced my work as well as the work of others being taken advantage of. I've been in situations where I had less social power and privilege than the other people involved and I was either afraid to ask for more out of fear of losing any potential opportunities, or told no, or given the runaround, or ignored when I did ask for more. This occurred even though I was contributing a significant amount of valuable time, energy, and knowledge. I was valued enough to be used as a resource, but not valued enough to be compensated for my contributions. Extracting labor from people without appropriate compensation perpetuates the status quo that tells people they have to prove themselves before they're worthy of being paid to do the work they're already doing. I believe we should set the standard for ourselves from the beginning, rather than subscribe to incremental external validation. This means you also need to honor other people's boundaries, which is why I believe it's important to learn what matters to the people you engage and connect with. A key to honoring your boundaries, honoring other people's boundaries, and helping them honor yours is communication. This is why I believe it's necessary to get rooted in the relationship you have with yourself so that you understand what you need, value, and expect from yourself as well as others.

When it comes to inclusive practices, you can expect that you may make some mistakes. So when you do make a mistake (because you will, that's the reality of being human) and someone brings it to your attention, that is a form of setting a boundary as well. Avoid minimizing or dismissing someone who is brave enough to share when they recognize and communicate the impact of a mistake that you have made.

Actionable Reflections:

Your Magic + Core Values = Natural Energy

When you tune into your natural energy, the connections you make should feel complimentary to who you are, which will lead you to build more genuine relationships that will help you thrive.

1. What type of energy do you embody?

   _____

   _____

   _____

2. What lights you up and makes you want to engage?

   _____

   _____

   _____

3. What do people say about their experiences with you and how you show up?

   _____

   _____

   _____

4. How can you translate this into the way you connect with people?

_____

_____

_____

5. *Why* do you do what you do?

_____

_____

_____

6. *What* are you really doing for people (go deeper, don't just say I'm a web designer...what do you do for people to make their lives easier?)

_____

_____

_____

7. How do you do what you do?

_____

_____

_____

8. Who do you do it for?

_____

_____

_____

9. What are your values?

_____

_____

_____

10. Are there causes or movements you support?

_____

_____

_____

As you seek out connections, who are your people and what are they like?

1. What kind of people do you want to surround yourself with?

    _____

    _____

    _____

2. What qualities and values do they have?

    _____

    _____

    _____

3. Do they support any causes or movements?

    _____

    _____

    _____

4. How do other people speak about them?

    _____

    _____

    _____

5. What are they doing for other people?

_____

_____

_____

Remember:
- Find Community
- Reach out
- Engage
- Share Your Story
- It's okay to say 'no'
- Check in with how you feel
- Speak up when something doesn't feel right
- Honor other people's boundaries
- Communicate
- Learn what matters to the people you engage with
- Avoid minimizing or dismissing people when they share their boundaries

CHAPTER 10

Creating Belonging

"True belonging only happens when we present our authentic, imperfect selves to the world, our sense of belonging can never be greater than our level of self-acceptance."

–Brene Brown

When you use your role and influence to ensure that everyone has a voice at the table, you're creating space for people to share and develop a sense of belonging. When people don't have to spend their mental and emotional energy wondering if they're welcome in a space, it leaves more room for creative thinking that leads to collaboration and new ideas. So really, when we're genuinely, intentionally inclusive, everyone wins. When you think about how everything ties into your role as an individual, you can bring it together to form your personal philosophy. You can download a free Personal Philosophy Statement Guide at BraveLeadershipChoice.com. The purpose of creating a personal philosophy that is specifically tied to inclusion is so you can take the time to really consider how inclusion and community take shape through the lens of your core values, your commitments to the causes/movements/organizations you support, and the way you want people to feel while interacting with you.

I believe we all have a responsibility to use our roles to create brave spaces through more human-focused awareness and mindful interactions where people can find a sense of belonging. I believe in being patient and taking the time to listen to the ideas and experiences of people in the social environments we interact in, so we can meet people where they are. Communication, compassion, and curiosity are vital to forming connections that foster growth and understanding between individuals with different lived experiences. I believe communities should be genuinely welcoming and inclusive. Here's the thing, peace and belonging can empower people with the trust and confidence they need to embody their purpose. And that's why I'm so committed to co-creating safety in the communities and environments I'm a part of by raising awareness and being receptive to feedback. I believe we all have the power to create brave spaces. They're created when we decide to expand our focus from the individual to the collective.

Start thinking about how your core values and beliefs can be incorporated into your role(s). Take some time to go through all of the work you've done so far, consider your goals for creating a positive impact. Then consider how you can communicate your commitment to inclusion and empower the social environments where you have influence. Once you've done this, you can outline your commitment in said environments.

Engage With Compassion

As you incorporate the practices you've learned about, remember to engage with compassion. We all have different lived experiences and it's important to create brave spaces that allow opportunities for people to show up as their whole selves. Be present and practice active listening in conversations. Show empathy. Let people know that you care about who they are and what they have going on. Acknowledge people for who they are and the value they have, and remember that people and their experiences matter. I think India Arie said it best during a talk she gave on Oprah's Super Soul Conversations, "You matter, because you exist." And I believe this quote from India Arie is relevant for both self-reflection and building relationships with people. We all matter and everyone deserves to engage in relationships where they can be seen, heard, and understood. We need to practice it for ourselves, so that we can model it for others. This is how we build aligned relationships and cultivate inclusive communities where people can feel a sense of belonging.

Create Space to Share

There's an Equity Consultant named Aiko Bethea who shared two questions on a podcast interview she did with Brene Brown which have proven to be effective tools for opening up dialogue when calling people in. This is for you to have in the back of your mind to consider using when you notice things being said or done that are harmful towards another person or group.

First, ask why...
"Why did you say or do that?"

Allow the other person time to respond.

Then ask why again...
"Why do you believe/do that?"

Allow them time to respond again.

Then, if you want to take it further, you can ask if they're aware of how what was said/done is harmful. These three questions create space for people to share their perspective while also opening up a dialogue with an opportunity to learn. The person asking the questions can gain more understanding of the other person's perspective and the person answering the questions can, hopefully, get an opportunity to repair any harm done. It also works well if you're trying to learn about something as long as you're mindful not to put people in the space of doing educational labor.

Be patient with yourself as you integrate this work and remember that practicing inclusion is a journey, not a destination. You may make mistakes along the way and the most important thing to be mindful of is how you handle those mistakes. If you choose to be receptive to feedback intended to help you learn and grow, your journey will begin to feel more automatic compared to those who choose to operate from a place of defensiveness. Remember that people who choose to bring things to your awareness are making an effort to support you in those moments.

If someone is brave, honest, and vulnerable enough to share their experience or knowledge, it is harmful to respond dismissively or tell them what they *should do* to make a situation more comfortable for you. It's already uncomfortable to bring a delicate topic to light. Bypassing the issue to center your perspective, deny what they're sharing is harmful, or demand education without fully listening to what is being shared erases any and all feelings of safety. This creates more harm and widens the gap for opportunities for everyone to feel welcome in a space.

When someone brings an issue to your attention, listen and allow space for them to share all of their thoughts and feelings without interrupting them. When it's your turn to speak, ask questions, but ask them calmly with compassion. Breathe if you feel uncomfortable (no matter which side of the conversation you're on). Difficult conversations are challenging to engage in, but they don't have to feel combative. Recognize what the person raising the issue does in response to your reaction and ask yourself if a real solution was reached. If the answer is 'no,' there's a good chance you caused harm and the person raising the issue no longer felt safe or supported to continue and protecting themselves was prioritized over helping you to do better. Express gratitude to the person for being vulnerable enough to share their experience and knowledge. This work is extremely challenging and extending appreciation for the effort that goes into continuously showing up in potentially harmful situations is always appreciated. People don't get to simply compartmentalize or take their work hats off when the work is focused on improving the lived experiences of human beings who have been marginalized, demonized, traumatized, turned into caricatures, and more. The work is literally everywhere and it costs continuous energy and awareness. This work is done out of *love*. Please remember that.

Actionable Reflections:

- Engage with compassion
- Create space to share
- Create brave spaces for people to be their whole selves
- Remember that everyone has a different lived experience
- Be present in your interactions
- Honor the reality that people matter because they exist

Download the Personal Philosophy Statement guide at BraveLeadershipChoice.com

What are 3-5 commitments you plan to practice to ensure inclusive, healthy social environments that promote bravery, safety, curiosity, open communication, learning, growth, creativity, collaboration, feedback, and belonging?

_____

_____

_____

_____

_____

_____

ACKNOWLEDGMENTS

I first want to acknowledge myself for committing to and completing this project. I have poured my heart, mind, and spirit into this and it would not have been possible without the wonderful people who encouraged and supported me along the way...

My oldest, very dear friend, Nick, who reviewed and sat through hours of preliminary presentations in the early development of my work.

My best friend, Jackie, whom I've had countless conversations with about navigating challenging interpersonal dynamics in our lives.

My dear friend, Paige, who has been my biggest cheerleader throughout the entire process of developing my framework and writing this book.

My friend, Leah Weinberg for sharing her own experience and advice with the writing and self-publishing process.

Jennifer Rappo, of Rappo Consulting, who was the first coach I made a significant investment in, who created the coaching container I needed to launch The Aligned Values Framework™ in an online course.

Kirstie Wheeler, friend and Professor at Berklee College of Music, who piloted The Aligned Values Framework™ in a college-level class and continues to use it in her business and classrooms.

Everyone who contributed by sharing their perspective on incorporating mindful practices:

- Tanisha Rodriguez
- Dr. Portia Jackson-Preston
- Cory Quailes
- Lara Estrada
- Lyvonne Briggs
- Kaig Lightner
- Monique Melton
- Paige Ray
- Erin Perkins

Everyone who read and provided feedback on the drafts:

- Leah Weinberg
- Paige Ray
- Laura Fennell
- Nick Molano
- Tamiah Bantum
- Carrie Murray

Everyone who has invested in this work by hiring me to host classes or guide them through my framework, co-creating, and fine-tuning along the way.

Huge thank you to my editor, Nailah Harvey, for her patience, attention to detail, perspective and feedback through the editing process.

Special thanks to Mayanthi Jayawardena for her beautiful book cover and website logos that illustrate the vision of intersecting colors, layered and woven to represent the winding intersections of identity and peaks and valleys of navigating this work.

Thanks to E. Mackey, for designing the book website.

ADDITIONAL RESOURCES AND EDUCATORS

Books:

Do Better: Spiritual Activism for Fighting and Healing from White Supremacy by Rachel Ricketts

Atlas of the Heart by Brene Brown

Learn Lead Lift: How to Think, Act and Inspire Your Way to Greatness by Wendy Ryan

The Antiracist Business Book by Trudi Lebron

Heal Your Way Forward: The Co-conspirator's Guide to An Antiracist Future by Myisha T. Hill

Educators:

Monique Melton - Anti-racism Educator, Shine Bright School

Jordan A. Maney - Social Justice, Joy, and Rest Educator, The Radical Joy Coach

Erin Perkins - Accessibility Educator, Mabley Q

Kirsten Ott Palladino - LGBTQ+ Educator, Equally Wed

Dr. Portia Jackson Preston, PhD - TedX Speaker and Equity-minded Wellness, Holistic Well-being, and Sustainable Work Practices, Empowered to Exhale

Katie Kurtz, MSW LISW-S - Trauma Informed Care Specialist

David Ryan Castro-Harris - Restorative Justice Educator, Amplify RJ

Nicole Cardoza - Anti-racism and Social Justice Educator, Anti-racism Daily

Tony Nabors - Racial Equity Insights

GLOSSARY

Ableism: Discrimination and exclusion towards people with mental, emotional, and/or physical abilities.

Action Bias: A need to act and develop solutions before a problem is defined or understood to feel good about taking action, even if it doesn't solve the problem.

Accessibility: Being easy to obtain or use (i.e., providing access for people with disabilities).

Anti-racist: Opposing racism and promoting racial tolerance.

Bias: Conscious or unconscious prejudice against individuals or groups based on their identity.

BIPOC: Black, Indigenous, People of Color.

Brand Statement: Defines an organization's mission, vision, goals, brand promise, core values, and beliefs.

Brave Space: Honors and invites people to show up fully in their humanity to be vulnerable while also creating space to address any potential harm or oppressive behavior that may arise and need to be addressed.

Character: The mental and moral qualities distinctive to an individual.

Code Switching: The practice of alternating between two or more languages or varieties of language. (For example, Black people who use African-American Vernacular English outside of professional environments changing their vernacular in certain environments to avoid being considered 'unprofessional' or discredited.)

Colorism: Differential treatment based on skin color, especially favoritism toward those with a lighter skin tone and mistreatment or exclusion of those with a darker skin tone, typically among those of the same racial group or ethnicity.

Connection: A relationship in which a person, thing, or idea is linked or associated with someone or something else—often influenced by or related to social environments.

Core Values: Guiding principles and foundational beliefs used to help define a brand.

Cultural Appropriation: The adoption or co-opting, usually without acknowledgment, of cultural identity markers associated with or originating in minority communities by people or communities with a relatively privileged status.

Diversity: The inclusion of individuals representing more than one national origin, color, religion, socioeconomic stratum, sexual orientation, etc.

Educational Labor: The act of expecting or demanding education from people with marginalized identities to help create an understanding of their culture, customs, lived experiences, practices, or traditions.

Equity: The quality of being fair or impartial (i.e., equal access and opportunity for advancement).

Inclusion: The act or policy of providing equal access to opportunities and resources for people who might otherwise be excluded based on the grounds of age, gender identity, race, class, sexual orientation, ability, etc.

Internalized Oppression: The acceptance of the beliefs or internalization of harmful misinformation spread by dominant groups in society by the marginalized and oppressed groups who are targeted.

Intersectionality: The interconnected nature of social categorizations such as race, class, and gender as they apply to a given individual or group, regarded as creating overlapping and interdependent systems of discrimination or disadvantage.

LGBTQ+: Lesbian, gay, bisexual, transgender, queer or questioning, +(plus) to indicate IAP; intersex, asexual, polyamorous.

Microaggression: A subtle but offensive comment or action directed at a minority or other non-dominant group that is often unintentional or unconsciously reinforces a stereotype (e.g., "I don't see you as Black").

Mission Statement: Defines what an organization does, why it exists, who it serves, and its overall goal (i.e., what you do, why you do it, who you do it for, what they get).

Oppression: Unjust or cruel exercise of authority or power.

Personal Philosophy Statement: Defines an individual's commitment to their community through their core values and beliefs.

Representation: The state or fact of being so represented (e.g., to demand representation on a board of directors).

Social environment: The environment developed by people, related to individuals, communities, and organizations, where interactions occur.

Spiritual bypassing: A "tendency to use spiritual ideas and practices to sidestep or avoid facing unresolved emotional issues, psychological wounds, and unfinished developmental tasks." –John Welwood

Status quo: An existing state of affairs, particularly regarding social or political issues; can demonstrate a resistance to change.

Tokenism: The practice or policy of making no more than a token effort or gesture, as in offering opportunities to minorities equal to those of the majority.

Vision Statement: Defines the future of an individual, organization, or brand, (i.e., where you want to be in 3-5 years).

Way of being: The language people use, the thoughts and emotions they experience, the physiological reactions that take place in the body and how they translate to an individual's behavior.

White centering: Puts the feelings, comfort, and well-being of white people above those of the groups that have been harmed and oppressed by white supremacy.

White supremacy: The belief that white people constitute a superior race and should therefore dominate society, typically to the exclusion or detriment of other racial and ethnic groups, in particular Black or Jewish people.

White washing: Taking practices, traditions, and teachings of non-white communities and making them more palatable and comfortable for white people.

WOC: Woman/women of color.

Let's Connect

Visit BraveLeadershipChoice.com for downloadable resources and learn more about The Aligned Values Framework™.

Learn more about Crystal and invite her to speak at BraveLeadershipChoice.com.

ABOUT THE AUTHOR

Crystal Whiteaker (pronouns: she/her) is an Inclusive Branding and Leadership Development and Consultant specializing in coaching and consulting for brands and leaders that care deeply about diversity, equity, inclusion, and belonging. Crystal brings over 15 years of creative, relational, process driven experience across multiple industries. An advocate for inclusive, human-focused, trauma informed leadership practices, Crystal is a self-described "corporate trained, creative hippie" who puts a strong focus on core values. Her purpose is to help people connect, communicate and lead with compassion, clarity and confidence. When she's not working, Crystal enjoys spending time at the beach, connecting with people, and exploring new places.

CPSIA information can be obtained
at www.ICGtesting.com
Printed in the USA
LVHW020114100423
743900LV00002B/257